African Traditional Religion versus Christianity

African Traditional Religion versus Christianity

Some Semiotic Observations

DMITRY USENCO

RESOURCE *Publications* · Eugene, Oregon

AFRICAN TRADITIONAL RELIGION VERSUS CHRISTIANITY
Some Semiotic Observations

Copyright © 2020 Dmitry Usenco. All rights reserved. Except for brief quotations in critical publications or reviews, no part of this book may be reproduced in any manner without prior written permission from the publisher. Write: Permissions, Wipf and Stock Publishers, 199 W. 8th Ave., Suite 3, Eugene, OR 97401.

Resource Publications
An Imprint of Wipf and Stock Publishers
199 W. 8th Ave., Suite 3
Eugene, OR 97401

www.wipfandstock.com

PAPERBACK ISBN: 978-1-7252-7160-9
HARDCOVER ISBN: 978-1-7252-7161-6
EBOOK ISBN: 978-1-7252-7162-3

Manufactured in the U.S.A. 05/18/20

Contents

Acknowledgements	vii
Introduction: The Background	1
Semiotics: A Science or a Mythology?	4
Case Study 1. Jesus and his Color in African Context	12
Case Study 2. Religious Buildings and Their Associative Links	14
Chapter I: Animality and Humanity—Nature and Culture	18
Chapter II: The Origin of Language	24
Chapter III: The Origin of Religion	30
Chapter IV: The Fall of Man	33
Chapter V: Reclaiming the Fetish	41
Case Study 3. The Fetish of the Akodessawa Market	42
Chapter VI: Rethinking the Idol	45
Chapter VII: Blood as Spiritual Currency	50
1. Cain and Abel	52
2. Ywa Dɛnsu	54
3. Execution on Calvary	55
Chapter VIII: Witchcraft	57
Chapter IX: Polytheism and Monotheism: Absorption vs Diffusion	63
1. Absorption	64
2. Diffusion	69
3. Holy Tuesday	72
4. Spy Wednesday	73
Chapter X: The Twilight of the Gods	76
Case Study 4. Nyame	80

Chapter XI: Lighting the Twilight: Renewal vs Denial	86
Chapter XII: The Christs of Africa	95
Chapter XIII: The Semiotic Message of Jesus	99
Case Study 5. The Conversion of Kwame Bediako	105
Chapter XIV: The Conquest: Joshua vs Josiah	108
Chapter XV: Exclusivism	116
Chapter XVI: Inclusivism	123
Case Study 6. The Big House	129
Chapter XVII: Pluralism	132
1. Progress vs Conservatism	133
Case Study 7. The Cellar and the Cell Phone	135
2. Plenitude vs Deficiency	136
3. Linearity vs Circularity	138
Case Study 8. The Fada	139
Conclusion	145
Bibliography	147

Acknowledgments

I DEDICATE THIS BOOK to my wife Irina who has been my main source of inspiration and who has, just as importantly, agreed to take charge of most of our family's chores, allowing me to take some "time off" (which turned out to be much lengthier than originally planned) in order to devote myself entirely to my project. This book would never see the light, o my beloved, were it not for your faith in me and in my ability to produce something worthy of notice after almost twenty-five years of silently drudging on together towards a powerfully attractive but often unsteady light in the distance. Thank you also for allowing me to speak first, although I could accept that favor only on condition that I would later do everything in my power to let you express in writing your own message to the world—whenever you feel ready to do that.

My further thanks go to all those who contributed to the conception and execution of this book in their own, often very diverse, ways. First, thanks to Daniil Loshmanov, our family's almost lifetime friend, for making us meet his wife Anita who comes from Ghana and whose company supplied us with the first spark to ignite our interest in Africa which later materialized in our visit to that land. I am also very grateful to her for jotting down at my request the first reading list on African Traditional Religion, when I expressed my wish to get a flavor of that subject. I can see now how wise and relevant her choice of recommended books was and how crucial it was on many occasions in determining the goals of my further research.

Next, I would like to thank those who facilitated my first-hand acquaintance with Africa—Jolinaiko Eco Tours—whose founders, Cindy Noordermeer-Panou and her husband Apollo Panou, were instrumental in turning our third trip to Africa into an amazing discovery of local culture and local people, both Traditionalists and Christians. A special word of thanks to the guide they provided to us, whose name—Isaac Aziawo—is worth inscribing in golden letters in our travel notes. The chap managed to do the impossible: to let us have an idea what voodoo religion is by touring some parts of Ghana and especially his native Togo in less than two weeks. His love and knowledge of his homeland are boundless; his professionalism and organizing skills are beyond all praise. I take this occasion to send my greetings to all the exceptionally nice people we met in his native village of Davedi.

Last but not least, I am totally grateful to those who read the manuscript of this book and provided their valuable comments, and especially to three of them: Reverend Father Joop Visser, Richard F. Turner, and the Reverend Canon Dr Stephen Evans, who were also kind enough to provide their endorsements on the back cover of my book. Thanks for letting me hope that my work is not a complete failure and thanks for spotting in it certain thoughts and ideas that looked original to some of you. There is no greater reward for any author than to be made believe that his work has revealed something that escaped notice of other people before —never mind how modest that discovery may be!

Laindon, Essex, March 2020

Introduction

The Background

BOTH THE TITLE AND the subtitle of this book point to the way it should be treated—as a series of observations. It cannot claim to be anything more, as its author is by no means qualified to identify himself as anyone else but a mere observer. Indeed, I cannot promote this book as a piece of academic research, first of all because I do not belong to the Academia (I used to a long time ago, but I have irrevocably lost that connection). I cannot, therefore, guarantee that everything I am going to say—every thought, every guess or every conclusion this book contains—will be in strict compliance with the highest scholarly standards, i.e. substantiated by references to first-hand evidence, peer reviews, and an exhaustive bibliography that would list all the publications produced on the subject to date. I honestly admit that I cannot maintain these standards and that in such a situation I cannot claim the status of an adviser but only that of an observer. Yet, if this status will allow me, nonetheless, to express a couple of thoughts that have previously evaded the attention of the academic community, I shall be happy enough with that modest achievement and consider the goal of this book to be reached.

I have to add that I also, unfortunately, do not possess any qualifications (either official or unofficial ones) that could provide me with at least a partial excuse for meddling with the subject: I am neither African by birth, nor a practitioner of any traditional religion. Conversely and equally true, I am neither a Christian minister, nor a Christian missionary. Therefore, I cannot officially represent any organized religion. That means that I am not only an observer, I am also an outsider. However, such disqualifications can perhaps turn to my advantage if I say that the main subject of my research is not the doctrinal basis but the *relationship* between African Traditional Religion (ATR) on the one hand and Christianity on the other. Once this is conceded, one may say that in such circumstances my non-aligned status may assure a more impartial and uninvolved treatment of the subject.

In fact, it is exactly this circumstance that allows me somehow to hope that my book will be not entirely useless. It is quite possible that a couple of independent and detached observations can at least somewhat contribute to a better understanding of the above relationship and perhaps even outline a potential roadmap towards its improvement. I believe it is really appropriate to speak about improvement because the current state of that relationship does not look perfect to many observers, whoever they may be. Therefore, if any of the ideas discussed and defended in this book will suggest a better way forward as far as the case of "ATR vs Christianity" is concerned, I shall consider my ambitions fully satisfied.

At this point those who have taken the trouble to run through the table of contents may be already raising their eyebrows in bewilderment. The chap declares his modest aspirations and yet—look at some of the headings under which he arranges his so-called "observations," especially at the start of his book: "Animality and Humanity" to begin with, "The Origin of Language" to follow, and "The Origin of Religion" to crown it all. Surely, his ambitions do not look so modest as he pretends!

I admit that it is a fair point and I want to do my best to provide an acceptable apology. I can start by quoting Jacque Derrida (1930–2004) who says that " . . . it is a necessary fact that empirical investigation quickly activates reflection upon essence."[1] Now, Derrida is, of course, a very controversial thinker and we shall come back to him later, in the methodological part of this introduction. Meanwhile, I find him to be absolutely right in this respect. It is really quickly, sometimes even too quickly, that dealing with a relatively minor issue causes the author to switch from particular to essential, to go upstream in an attempt to discover the source, and to draw his premises as well as conclusions *ex ipse fonte*. In other words, I find this widespread habit to slip into generalities very human and therefore pardonable. In most cases, the author simply tries to tell his readers where he[2]

---

1. Derrida, *Of Grammatology*, 75.

2. All instances of impersonal use of personal pronouns follow the old-fashioned "he" pattern. Thus, "he" is consistently used when any human being is meant in general without reference to a specific individual. "Man" is usually preferred to "human being" and "God" is always replaced by "he." In answer to the question how such a usage agrees with the prevailing idea of gender equality, I would like to declare that I *am* a feminist (provided that my belonging to the male gender does not disqualify me from being

stands on a specific issue, if only for clarity's sake. This *ascension* towards the source is reflected in the titles of some chapters of my book. I hope the appropriateness of their designations becomes evident later.

An analogy-based elucidation may be here appropriate. In the early centuries of Christianity, when the consensus on its main dogmas and doctrines was still to be achieved, every priest and preacher, before presenting a sermon or a message he had in store for his audience, would mount the pulpit and briefly state what his stand was on the main controversial points of the religion he professed. In other words, he would present his *creed*. The practice of saying the creed has survived to our days in Christian liturgy even though it has, over centuries, become more of a formality than any conscious act of declaring one's religious convictions. But I think that nothing prevents anyone from reviving that practice in its original usage and begin his book with stating the most essential points on which it rests.

Please note that by saying so I do not mean that I intend to discuss, much less argue against, any established tenets of Christianity or some other religion—they are simply not my concern here. I am not going to discuss the existence of God, the veracity of Christian revelation or the alleged deficiencies of traditional religion. I am not a theologian and I am well aware that I am too much advanced in my years even to attempt becoming one. The words "*Vita brevis, ars longa*" are true, of course, about any branch of human knowledge, but when it comes to *ars theologica*, I would have no doubts to characterize it as the *longissima*. Instead of theology I have decided to go for semiotics, and my choice of method, as I hope to show later, should be adequate to the modest objectives this study pursues. I also believe I am better qualified for the role of a semiotician because I have a degree in linguistics and another one (although slightly less relevant) in literature. Finally, I hope that my fairly recently acquired passion for Africa will at least partially excuse (if not compensate for) the gaps in my fundamental knowledge.

A statement of creed it may be, still it cannot evade the question: Why make it so long, spanning the first three chapters—something that could perhaps be fitted into this introduction? My answer is that such a feat would

---

one, from some extremist point of view). A feminist I am, but I also believe there are better ways of expressing one's adherence to feminism other than using such newspeak formations as "he/she," "he or she," "she or he," "(s)he," "they" (when in fact you refer to a single person) or simply "she" (when a patriarchal-minded traditionalist would expect "he"). Most of these usages, compared to other European languages which I am at least partially familiar with, are possible in English only. Another analogy can also help to illustrate the point: thus, I believe there are better ways of proving, for example, that one is a Christian, other than wearing a cross around one's neck or carrying a rosary at all times and places.

be easier for a theologian than for a semiotician to accomplish. The Nicene Creed is indeed an exceptionally brief document, but we know too well at what price that brevity was purchased—at the cost of centuries-long debates, arguments, compromises and eventual reconciliations. Every line of that deceitfully short text conceals hundreds of volumes in comments, justifications, apologies and anathemas.

But once again, this is not a theological work and formulating a creed which has never gone through any rigorous debate by experts in the field would certainly be a more difficult job which is likely to result in a much more convoluted statement. This is especially true for semiotics—a discipline which, very much unlike theology, has still a long way to go until it reaches even a weak semblance of maturity. As for semiotics of religion, this discipline can be regarded to be still in its infancy (those who are interested in details can find some in the next section). What follows from such a state of affairs? Certainly more chance for all sorts of marginals like me but on the other hand more onerous requirements to provide a more comprehensive prolegomena to a discipline which for many people still retains a strong savor of esoterism. Thus I believe to have done my best to come up with some sort of "general principles" in the first three chapters. If the reader finds that such a protracted overture could be made shorter, I will be more than happy if he shows me a way to do it.

Semiotics: A Science or a Mythology?

A brief disclaimer first: If the reader finds the coming section irrelevant, boring or incomprehensible, he may feel free to abandon reading it at any time and go straight to the case studies that follow. I can assure the reader that I shall bear him no grudge for that. After all, I consider the case studies to be the most important part of this book, for the well-known reason that one straight example is worth a whole volume of theoretical circumlocutions. The methodological principles of my work should become intuitively clear from what I am going to say later. Yet the reader who is curious to know what sort of "schematics" is hidden behind my "interface" is encouraged to read on.

As the subtitle of this book makes clear, the method chosen here is *semiotic*. As I said in the previous section, my choice of method has been predetermined by my belief that I cannot claim theology to be within the scope of my scholarly competence. However, I also believe that semiotics can be a feasible and an easier alternative, especially when it comes to approaching religion from a nonpartisan point of view, i.e. without the need to identify oneself as an adherent of Christianity, African traditionalism or any other religion. But what do I understand by semiotics? The word (and the discipline it denotes) may sound new or not quite familiar to some of my readers and invite some further explanation.

Well, semiotics, as its very name implies,[3] is *a study of signs*. Defined this way, it appears a to be perfectly legitimate epistemological tool. We are surrounded by signs and understanding them should help us discern the best way to interact with our surroundings. Religion therefore makes a legitimate target of semiotic research because religion can obviously be also approached as a *system of signs*. This seems especially true if the sign is defined in the broadest possible sense, the way it is done by one the founding fathers of semiotics, Charles Sanders Peirce (1839–1914) who virtually identifies *thought* with *sign*. Specifically, this is what he writes in the article entitled "Questions Concerning Certain Facilities Claimed for Man" (1868):

> If we seek the light of external facts, the only cases of thought which we can find are of thought in signs. Plainly, no other thought can be evidenced by external facts. But we have seen that only by external facts can thought be known at all. The only thought, then, which can possibly be cognized is thought in signs. But thought which cannot be cognized does not exist. All thought, therefore, must necessarily be in signs.[4]

Quite typical of most founding fathers from past ages (with Socrates, Jesus and Buddha in that company) Peirce never wrote comprehensively on the subject of semiotics, leaving to posterity only a handful of passing remarks scattered throughout his writings on other topics. It is impossible to tell how much he would agree or disagree with the inferences drawn from his works by his ever-multiplying disciples (not all of whom he would probably acknowledge). Yet, as long as we agree that the above quotation can be read literally (and not as some disguised moral allegory) I think it would be appropriate to counter it with the following question: If we are capable of thinking in signs only, would it not mean that every time we consciously interrelate with the outside world, we merely engage in an endless process of signification? Would not it suggest that by conveniently reducing our cognition to a set of signs we may miss the true essence of things, something that lurks behind and beyond the "painted veil"? Is our sign little more than a visual or audial image, a cartoon that sketches objects snatched from outside only with only a remote degree of approximation?

---

3. From the Greek *sema*—sign
4. Peirce, *Peirce on Signs*, 49.

Any reductionism is dangerous, of course, because it can lead to a distorted or lopsided view of reality. Having been a student of Victorian Literature in the past, I know one especially vivid example of reductionism from another field—political economy—brilliantly satirized by John Ruskin in *Unto This Last* (1860). In the quotation below, the object of his derision is the conventional notion of "economic person" actively promoted in the nineteenth century by the followers of Adam Smith and David Ricardo who, by the way, retain their status of classics of economic thought to this day:

> Observe, I neither impugn nor doubt the conclusions of the science, if its terms are accepted. I am simply uninterested in them, as I should be in those of a science of gymnastics which assumed that men had no skeletons. It might be shown, on that supposition, that it would be advantageous to roll the students up into pellets, flatten them into cakes, or stretch them into cables; and that when these results were effected, the re-insertion of the skeleton would be attended with various inconveniences to their constitution. The reasoning might be admirable, the conclusions true, and the science deficient only in applicability. Modern political economy stands on a precisely similar basis. Assuming, not that the human being has no skeleton, but that it is all skeleton, it founds an ossifiant theory of progress on this negation of a soul; and having shown the utmost that may be made of bones, and constructed a number of interesting geometrical figures with death's-heads and humeri, successfully proves the inconvenience of the reappearance of a soul among these corpuscular structures. I do not deny the truth of this theory: I simply deny its applicability to the present phase of the world.

This is a serious objection, but I believe that Ruskin's reproach of "negation of a soul" does not apply to semiotics. I think we can argue along the following lines:

Sign is unique—in the sense that its nature is to unite, not to divide; it is synthetic, not analytical; holistic, not reductionist. This time our arguments will come not from Pierce but from the other founding father of semiotics, Swiss linguist Ferdinand de Saussure (1857–1913). That scholar, even more in accordance with the paternal tradition outlined above, left to posterity absolutely nothing on the subject in his own writings—all we have at our disposal are the notes taken by his students during his lectures, which they later collected, collated and published to the best of their editorial abilities. With respect to Saussure we know even less to what extent he would approve the conclusions that we draw from his posthumously published

Course in General Linguistics (1916). Yet some things can be inferred with greater certainty than others. One of those issues on which variant readings do not seem to exist is his teaching about the nature of linguistic sign (which by extension can be extrapolated to any other sign in general). According to Saussure, every sign possesses two essential components which exist in an inseparable unity yet always point in opposite directions. He calls them "*le signifié*" and "*le significant,*" the signified and the signifier. The former refers to the idea (command, address, information etc.) expressed or transmitted in communication; the latter relates to the medium though which that expression is made (it can be a word, a gesture, a picture or anything of the kind). Thus the sign (any sign, not necessarily a linguistic one) by virtue of its very nature, accomplishes the otherwise impossible mission of combining within itself the spiritual and the material, the soul and the corpuscular structure.

This is a perfect antidote against reductionism. It supplies an invaluable tool that allows us to approach any phenomenon of human culture (religion not excepted) in its unity and plenitude, rendering its due equally to body and soul. Yet the euphoria we feel at our first discovery of Saussurean semiotics is short-lived. The next thing that Saussure says is that the relation between the signified and the signifier is purely *arbitrary*. We call a spade "a spade" for no special reason, other than common usage. But to say that the relationship between the two things is based on random chance is to deny, in fact, the very existence of that relationship. We are thus left with an even worse reductionism where the connection between body and soul is compacted to a mere mechanical cohabitation. Paradoxically, in reverse perspective, we end up with a religious (mythical/mystical) rather than a scientific category. Here it would be pertinent to remember the most widely accepted etymology of "religion" which derives it from the Latin *religare*— "to link." In Saussure's version, the signified and the signifier seem to get linked with each other by means of a magical *fiat*, with no further inquiry possible. Can anything be done about it, so that the constitution of the sign looks a bit more meaningful?

Saussure himself was adamant in denying even the possibility to pose that question. However, even he was probably having a gut feeling that such a non-binding relationship, based entirely on chance, stands in marked contrast with the rest of his system which in all other respects is very rigidly deterministic. Yet, instead of trying to do something about this inconsistency, Saussure preferred to expel it from his mind using the well-known technique which Sigmund Freud (1856–1939) usually calls "compulsion prohibition." Freud also suggests that in anthropological terms this psychic phenomenon can be viewed as tantamount to imposing a taboo.[5] This once again arouses a suspicion that we deal with a mythical, rather than a scientific solution.

Here is a quotation from the *Course in General Linguistics*. It obviously refers to language but is perfectly applicable to any sign system in general (including, obviously, religion):[6]

> Language at any given time involves an established system and an evolution. At any given time, it is an institution in the present and a product of the past. At first sight, it looks very easy to distinguish between the system and its history, between what it is and what it was. In reality, the connection between the two is so close that it is hard to separate them. Would matters be simplified if one considered the ontogenesis of linguistic phenomena, beginning with a study of children's language, for example? No. It is quite illusory to believe that where language is concerned the problem of origins is any different from the problem of permanent conditions. There is no way out of the circle.[7]

The concluding phrase of the quoted paragraph is indeed exemplary. Saussure is so unwilling to step out of the magic circle he has so conveniently drawn around himself, that he is even ready to sacrifice common sense by claiming that "ontogenesis" and "permanent condition" are one and the same thing. Thus the taboo he imposes on enquiring into the origin of language necessitates the creation of another myth—the one which says that the difference between past and present is irrelevant.

This is not the only mytheme discoverable in Saussure. Another one given below is perhaps even more illuminating. Saussure's critics have repeatedly pointed out that the names he uses for the two components (*signifié—signifiant*) look very similar, barely distinguishable from each other.[8] Why does he do that, considering how important it might seem to draw a clear distinction here? The answer, which after the previous quotation will probably no longer look so controversial, is that we can view this near-identity in the light of another myth. Specifically, this is the myth of *divine twins*, of which Castor and Pollux, the Dioscuri, are perhaps the best-known

---

5. Freud, *Totem and Taboo*, 37.

6. "Especially to religion" I would say, for, as I argue later, language and religion have a common origin.

7. Saussure, *Course in General Linguistics*, 9.

8. This near-identity is lost in the above-quoted translation by Harris who instead uses the terms "signification" and "signal." Apparently, the translator attempts to improve Saussure by means of demythologizing him. I am not sure whether he thus renders a service or a disservice to the father of semiotics.

example. In fact, the myth exists in numerous varieties all over the world. Its main theme is, however, invariably the same: there are two twins of which only one is divine, the other one being mortal.[9] Quite in compliance with their heterogenous natures, the two usually co-exist in an uneasy relationship which often involves envy, enmity, deception, sometimes even murder or at least manslaughter, as in the well-known example of the legendary founders of Rome—Remus and Romulus (originally simply "Romus")—whose very similarity of names is almost built on the Saussurean pattern. Yet occasionally, the twins may move to make up, which can involve concessions and even self-sacrifice. Thus Pollux, the divine member of the couple, sacrifices half of his immortality in favor of his brother after the latter is mortally wounded by their foes. The forces of simultaneous repulsion and attraction that exist between such twins find a good match in the Saussurean sign whose one component is immaterial ("divine") while the other ("the mortal one") provides a link with earthly realities for the former. As far as their interrelationship is concerned, its main unease comes mostly from the allegedly arbitrary character of that connection.

Saussure's mythology has proven catchy and resilient. This is evident from the fact that a whole generation of scholars that followed on the heels of Saussure—commonly known as *structuralists*—have respectfully observed his taboo, never violating the sanctity of the arbitrariness principle. Those who later tried to outgrow Saussure's dominance—commonly known as *poststructuralists*—often overestimated their success. I do not want to bore the reader with a detailed review of all forms which their struggle for independence took in the twentieth century.[10] I shall limit myself to one example. I am going, as promised, to bring Jacque Derrida once more onto the stage.

In the book I have already quoted (*Of Grammatology*), Derrida reserves a considerable space for exposing the philosophical inconsistencies of Saussure. No wonder, for Saussure *does* have plenty of them, and only a

---

9. An exhaustive account of this myth is contained in the brilliant study titled *Boanerges* by J. Rendel Harris, a must-read for anyone who intends to delve into the "twin problem." Among other things, the book abounds in African material.

10. This knowledge can be obtained from various readily available "introductions for beginners," for example *Semiotics: A Graphic Guide* by Paul Cobley and Litza Jansz, or simply from the relevant article on Wikipedia. As for the semiotics of religion, I managed to locate only two fairly up-to-date publications. *Semiotics of Religion: Signs of the Sacred in History* by Robert A. Yell (2013) is a conscientious book which, unfortunately does not stand up to its title as it concentrates on relatively marginal religious phenomena (incantations, rhetorical devices etc.). *A Semiotic Approach to the Theology of Inculturation* by Cyril Orji can serve as a good compendium of the work previously done by other semioticians but, alas, not much else.

truly devoted admirer of the Genevan professor would overlook or ignore them. Besides, Derrida was a professional philosopher—something that Saussure never was. I am sure that Derrida would have destroyed all my argumentation with a click of a finger if he had ever had a chance to come across it. Allow me humbly to proceed, all the same.

The whole discipline of "grammatology" as invented by Derrida is, basically, about one thing—the assertion that written speech *precedes* oral speech in the cultural development of human race. This is obviously an absurd idea and it remains such, up to the end of the book, in spite of all the ingenuity and eloquence which the author generously pours over its pages. The question which the reader cannot help asking in this situation is why Derrida needs all this casuistry which serves apparently no purpose. A closer look at his writing reveals, however, that such a purpose does exist. It is to promote the same Dioscurian concept of two heterogeneous twins, which we have observed in Saussure. Only this time a very particular version of this myth is promoted—the one that can be found in the Book of Genesis, the story of Jacob reclaiming his birth right (i.e. his priority status) from Esau.

Writing, in the ordinary sense of the word (i.e. the process effected with a pen and ink or their common predecessors and substitutes) is not, according to Derrida, a divine craft, it is a usurper—like Esau, in terms of his misappropriated primogeniture. The mystical arch-writing that precedes the invention of writing in the usual sense is, says Derrida, the true first-born offspring of humanity, which must regain its birth-right at any cost—like Jacob taking over from Esau in the Bible. Thus, Derrida's postmodernist grammatology still conceals an ancient myth in its core—a myth that has been a staple for generations of semioticians and is still serving their needs, even of the most rebellious ones—those who dare criticize the founding fathers.

But perhaps the reader would like to know my own opinion on this matter? My answer can sound a bit surprising or maybe not at all surprising—depending on the stand the reader himself has taken with respect to the issue discussed above. I find nothing wrong about studying signs by means of other signs. Please remember, I understand sign in the broadest possible sense—the way Peirce did. From this point of view, religion is just a special instance of signification. It is a "symbolic form" according to Ernst Cassirer (1874–1945) a philosopher of the pre-structuralist age. Certainly, symbol is a particular variety of sign. The only stipulation I advance at this juncture is as follows: While dealing with signs, symbols or myths, have courage to admit that you are engaging in an essentially symbolic/mythical activity.

This may sound unfair. This may look like casting out devils by the power of Beelzebub. The reference is, of course, to the Gospel (Matt 9:34;

Luke 11:15) but the simile itself comes from Søren Kierkegaard (1813–1855) who actually applies it to the poets.[11] I believe that the semioticians can be added to that cohort as well. I also believe that, unlike Jesus who denied this accusation thrown at him by Pharisees, the semiotician, just like the poet, would probably have to swallow it, admitting that his ultimate goal is not to destroy the devils whom he simply treats as another "symbolic form" but to compare them one with another. Is it not just as natural, he would say, as to compare different poems, advertisements or spells? A creation myth of some extinct race with a consumerist myth of modern Western society next to it, why not?

Why not indeed, but is it really enough? Is there actually no way to break free from the Saussurean circle? Are we so surely caged in an enclosed space where we can only think *in* signs *about* signs, without ever hoping to ascertain their provenance? My answer to this accursed question is: Yes, but only if we choose to respect the taboo imposed by Saussure and reinforced by his followers; if we obstinately stick to the arbitrariness principle; or, in broader terms, is we insist on staying within the positivist tradition of the late nineteenth century from which most of the classical twentieth-century semiotics derives. An alternative to that approach would be to adopt the position of naïve realism or to pay homage to its "divine twin"—philosophic idealism (of which Cassirer is only one representative). In figurative language that would generally mean going past the prohibitory sign erected by Saussure and cutting through the net woven by Derrida who calls it "text" in line with its etymological meaning (from the Latin *texere*—to weave, to join), going literally *hors-texte*. Most semioticians would brand such an attempt as "metaphysics"—a word that has acquired a strongly derogatory meaning in their school. Once again, I do not mind: if my method can be concisely styled as "metaphysical semiotics" (even though it sounds almost like an oxymoron), then be it so. I do not mean to say that most of my writing is not going to be still very close in appearance to the twentieth-century semiotic fundamentalism, but I reserve a right to be sometimes naively metaphysical without any further notice.

I hope I have done with theory and can now safely proceed to the "real thing," the actual subject matter of my research. I want to start with the following two case studies which, I hope, will give my readers a flavor of what to expect in the rest of the book and how semiotic method may work in practice. Both examples are taken from African realities although they rather deal with Christianity than traditional religion. However, in Africa, as some of my readers will surely know, the two things are often intertwined.

---

11. Kierkegaard, *Fear and Trembling*, chapter 3, §19.

Case Study 1. Jesus and his Color in African Context

I am tempted to start my presentation with the words "While travelling around Africa, I repeatedly saw . . . " but I suspect such a beginning may contain an overstatement. All my travels in Africa are limited to three fortnightly visits: two to Ghana (in 2016 and 2017) and one to Togo (in 2019). I am painfully aware that six weeks in total are not enough to authorize me to refer to Africa as a whole. To be absolutely correct, I would need to say "in some parts of West Africa" instead of simply "in Africa" whenever I speak about my personal experiences. I do not do so every time only because I want to save space. The only other thing I can say in my defense is that I have tried to compensate for the insufficiency of my "fieldwork" with a wider range of my reading which occasionally went beyond West Africa. Still, it is mostly Ghana and Togo that will remain the focus of this book. I do hope that everything I touch upon here is relevant for the whole of West Africa, but I apologize in advance if it does not turn out to be the case, at least on some occasions. Finally, I hope the reader will appreciate my being honest in revealing the potential abyss of my ignorance.

To resume—While travelling around some parts of West Africa, but especially in Ghana, I repeatedly saw various Christian churches advertising themselves on billboards by the roadside. Some of those adverts bore an image of Jesus Christ. A remarkable feature of his representation was that in nearly all those cases he was depicted as a very fair-skinned person, with the color of his hair even not always black. He emphatically displayed Western European, almost Nordic, features. The likeliest paragon for such depiction seems to be *Salvator Mundi* by Leonardo da Vinci.

This obviously goes against the historical truth. The real Jesus was a native of Palestine and should, by all probability, belong to the Mediterranean, rather than the Nordic race. He should have been dark-haired and swarthy-faced—there is absolutely nothing in the Gospel to suggest that he could have been an albino. Considering that he would spend a lot of time outdoors, under the scorching Galilean sun and that he was virtually homeless (Matt 8:20, Luke 9:58) he should have acquired an especially dark complexion. The question is: Why does this marked whiteness persist in representing Jesus in some parts of West Africa?

I can think of at least two different answers. It is quite possible that both of them are valid, depending on what predominates in the perception of Christ by Africans: either as a representative of the "white people's world" or as a symbol of something more genuinely transcendent. Let us consider both options.

1. Jesus as an idealized white man. This interpretation naturally comes to mind on seeing how Jesus is often presented in Africa. His emphatic whiteness may come from the fact that his origin is associated less with his actual birthplace than with the birthplace of those who brought him to West Africa—predominantly white European missionaries in the ninetieth century. Such a perception tends to ignore the fact that Europeans themselves are far from being racially uniform in their appearance (Nordic vs Mediterranean, Western European vs Eastern European etc.). The key piece of information is that *Jesus was white* and, once it is ascertained, the most "typical" variety of the white race is chosen for his representation.

2. Jesus as an expression of transcendence. This aspect will become obvious as soon as we turn our attention to the general significance of color white in African Traditional Religion (and many other world religions). White stands for the colorless and therefore, by extension, also for the invisible, the immaterial, the transcendent, the otherworldly etc. Hence the use of white powder in many African rituals that involve contact with the spirit world. However, such color connotation should also mean that a deity represented with paler complexion would be in a privileged position compared to a darker-colored one whose appearance would look less spiritual. Because Jesus is supposed to be "naturally" white, that puts him at an obvious advantage over indigenous African gods. This advantage has to be emphasized as much as possible by those who promote Jesus' superiority over traditional deities. Thus, from naturally white in real life he becomes unnaturally white in representation. Any attempt to replace it with an image of dark-skinned Jesus would feel, from this perspective, as an attempt to downgrade him to a lower, less spiritual and less transcendent deity. Christianity and Westernism thus seem to win in both scenarios—all thanks to color white, albeit at the expense of misrepresenting the appearance of historical Jesus.

At this stage I shall refrain from drawing any further conclusions from what we have just discussed. I want my readers to treat it simply as an illustration of the important role that color symbolism can play in a situation with different competing religions. I also wanted to show how semiotics can allow us to penetrate through the skin color and analyze its cultural significance without necessarily committing ourselves to any side.

Case Study 2. Religious Buildings and Their Associative Links

Church buildings in Western Europe and Africa, in spite of all their differences due to geography and climate, belong essentially to the same architectural style. As such, they account for one of the very few similarities between the two continents. The origin and evolution of their style is irrelevant for this study. Instead, we should rather concentrate upon the semiotic associations they evoke when looked upon.

Certainly, the appearance of most religious buildings makes them stand out among the surrounding structures both in Europe and Africa. They do so, however, in very different ways on the two different continents. Most churches in Europe are actually survivors from past centuries. Many of them have been desperately struggling over the past hundred years or so to prove their relevance for modernity. They manage to do so only with varying degrees of success. They are often surrounded by office buildings and shops whose bustling activity often stands in marked contrast with the "abomination of desolation" that many churches display, irrespective of the fact that many of them have the status of "listed buildings" and are officially protected by the state as objects of cultural significance. Yet, however well they may be looked after, they still often feel neglected and out of touch with contemporary reality. Europe, at least the western part of it, does not seem to need them any longer (not in the current numbers anyway) but is reluctant to admit it openly. Besides, many people there still perceive them as the most appropriate venues for weddings and funerals, even though for not much else.

Not so in Africa. Here many church buildings also stand out among the surrounding structures but semiotically point in a very different direction. Some of them date back to the colonial period but, unlike other samples of colonial architecture, they are not in a state of disrepair. In fact, churches are very often the only buildings that seem to be well looked after. As such, they may be perceived as the only well-to-do survivors of the colonial past. The new churches which keep springing up all over Africa, including those that no longer have connections with missionary projects, seem to impart the same idea—that of stability and substantiality, in contrast to their often squalid surroundings. In this capacity, they certainly evoke very different associations than they normally do in Europe. They can be regarded as a sign of Africa's aspirations towards economic and spiritual prosperity, of the times to come, when not only churches but everything else will look properly arranged, in harmony with the natural and social environment. But they may also suggest the idea that Africa's better future is inseparable from embracing Christianity.

Indeed, these samples of Africa's Christian architecture often stand in marked contrast with the appearance of its traditional temples and shrines which look like temporary structures compared to the monumentalism of churches. This leads to a more general question: Do the anticipated improvements in Africa's socioeconomic conditions necessarily imply the triumph of monumental style for religious buildings? How much does this idea agree with the African cultural heritage?

Monumental style in architecture may look reassuring of the future but, on the other hand, it may create an uneasy association with another archetypal symbol with an opposite meaning—the Tower of Babel. It may be worth remembering that the corresponding myth was born in circumstances quite similar to Africa's recent past. The Jews who redacted perhaps the best-known version of that story (as told in Genesis 11) were at that time kept captive by the Babylonians who, in modern idiom, can be regarded as their colonizers. The Babylonians were very fond of monumental architecture which for them probably symbolized their technical and managerial achievements, but which delivered a very different message to their oppressed prisoners who interpreted it as a sign of their captors' diabolical vanity and pride. Creating monumental buildings can, therefore, be viewed as man's attempt to rival God or even take His place. Such an endeavor is, of course, doomed to failure, creating nothing but misunderstanding and chaos, as symbolized by God's confounding of language.

We are also reminded at this point how unwilling the Hebrew God was to accept a permanent place of residence when it was offered to Him by King David:

> And it came to pass that night, that the word of the Lord came unto Nathan, saying, Go and tell my servant David, Thus saith the Lord, Shalt thou build me an house for me to dwell in? Whereas I have not dwelt in any house since the time that I brought up the children of Israel out of Egypt, even to this day, but have walked in a tent and in a tabernacle. In all the places wherein I have walked with all the children of Israel spake I a word with any of the tribes of Israel, whom I commanded to feed my people Israel, saying, Why build ye not me an house of cedar? (2 Sam 7:4–17)[12]

God who was previously content with nomadic lifestyle does not seem to like the prospect of being pinpointed to a particular spot. On the whole, such an attitude looks reasonable, considering that the figure of God without a fixed abode agrees quite well with this idea of his omnipresence as a monotheistic deity. On the other hand, God with a permanent place of residence may look restricted in his freedom or even impaired in his omnipotence.

---

12. All biblical quotations are, unless specially referenced, from the King James Authorised Version.

Of course, everyone knows that what was denied to David was accomplished by his successor Solomon who eventually had the temple built, apparently with God's blessing. However, some Bible readers may regard this project as a setback, rather than an advancement on the path of consistent monotheism, for Solomon, as it is also well-known, in many respects was simply motivated by the wish to imitate and rival the wonts and practices of the neighboring Egyptians who were obvious trendsetters at that time in the region. That, while trying to catch up with Egypt the Hebrew king also adopted the cults of certain pagan deities, is another well-known fact . . .

Nevertheless, the idea of an omnipresent "homeless" God remained alive and came into prominence again after the fall of the Jerusalem Temple (70 AD). Thus, the Gospel of John relocates the divine Word back into its old residence—the tabernacle (1:14), as testified by the word "*eskēnōsen*" used by the evangelist in the Greek original, which, in Young's Literal Translation, reads as "And the Word became flesh, and did tabernacle among us." This image of a "nomadic" God is fully seconded by the synoptic gospels where Jesus emphasizes his homelessness (already referred to in the previous case study) when he says in Matthew 8:20 and Luke 9:58, "The foxes have holes, and the birds of the air have nests; but the Son of man hath not where to lay his head." Is this saying simply a complaint that a prophet is not appreciated in his own country or does it point to some deeper metaphysical necessity for an incarnate God to be denied the privilege of settled and orderly life?

If the above speculations are at least partially true, it means that the shrines of indigenous deities commonly erected in Africa may look more adequate for housing their inhabitants just because they have a pronounced "makeshift" appearance. Viewed from that perspective, they can look more appropriate to house spiritual beings—ancestors and deities—who can be willing to accept such structure only as a short-term accommodation because their divine duties require them to be present at different sites—both in the earthly and the spiritual realm.

In the light of God's revelation to the Prophet Nathan, at least some Africans may have reasons to suspect that the pompous churches erected in the past by white people only testify to the latter's pride and conceit. Can it be that the sense of reassurance brought to Africa by Christianity is in fact nothing but ill-founded reliance on white man's alleged cultural and technical superiority that, in the long run, may bring nothing good except spiritual disintegration to the Africans? But also, can we suppose that similarly pompous structures currently raised by Africans themselves manifest the latter's wish to surpass their former masters in their pride and conceit? Once again, as in the previous case study, let us withhold a final answer until we acquire a better understanding of how different religious environments interact.

I hope that by now the reader has formed an idea of what my *observations* may look like further in this book. But first, as I have previously hinted, I would like to state in more general terms the theoretical assumptions that underlie them.

Chapter I

Animality and Humanity—Nature and Culture

As I have said in the Introduction, I would like to start from the very beginning, from the very source of humanity. This is not because I expect to make any discovery or even to say anything new. Rather, this is because I am not aware of any semiotic theory that would provide a sufficient coverage of this important subject—the semiotics of human nature as a whole, rather than its specific manifestations. Usually, when a semiotician starts his discourse, both language and culture are taken for granted as things already in existence. However, this only means that the approach of most semioticians to the problem of origins is intuitive, rather than fully analytical. I want to try parting with that tradition and attempt to introduce certain definitions and assumptions which will hopefully make all further discussion much more self-explanatory than is normally the case. How successful my enterprise will prove is for the reader to judge. Even if he finds that I do not sound very convincing, I can still be consoled by the thought that I simply feel more comfortable with that way of expressing myself.

Let us start with a definition of religion. Semiotically, it can be described as *a system of signs used to communicate and interact with what is believed to be the spiritual world*. We should bear in mind, however, that religion is part of a much broader phenomenon which is usually denoted as *culture*. From the same, semiotic, perspective, culture can be defined as *a comprehensive system of signs which distinguishes human beings from other animals*. It follows from this definition that culture is an exclusive possession of mankind and that we can put an equal sign between culture and humanity as such. It is defined as *comprehensive* because it includes not only religion but also other important aspects of human identity. Thus, apart from religion, other very important factors that differentiate man from beast are what we can call (rather simplistically for the purpose of this research) *technology* and *language*. I said "simplistically" because this division is quite subjective by itself and can be drawn along different lines by other researchers of culture. However, for the purposes of the current study, I find this conventional distinction helpful for reasons to be outlined below.

Etymology can be helpful. It is true that it can sometimes be also misleading because the original and current meanings of a given word often do not match. Yet the very gap between the two meanings can prove illuminating and point in the right direction. Let us see then how much it could be the case with *culture*. Its etymology is well-known. Ultimately, the word derives from the Latin "*colere*" which is usually translated as "to till the earth." So, it looks like the etymological meaning of "culture" simply equates it *agriculture*. At first sight, this may look misleading indeed. Firstly, it seems to reduce culture only to its material aspect, i.e. technology, which, as we have just mentioned, is only one of its constituent parts. Secondly, it places the origin of culture as late as the early Neolithic—the time when some peoples actually started to till the earth on an industrial basis. Yet we know very well that culture came into existence long before the rise of land cultivation and that the latter has never been universally adopted by mankind. Indeed, many nations did not choose agriculture as their main occupation and preferred to adhere to stock farming or to even more traditional hunting-gathering. Some of them stick to that choice to this day.

We shall come back to the topic of "agriculture vs. cattle breeding" (Cain vs Abel) in chapter VII when we talk about the nature of sacrifice in different religions. Right now, however, we can amplify the etymological meaning of culture and apply it not only to land cultivation but any type of cultivation, i.e. *any human interference that changes the natural order of things*, however slight and inconspicuous it may look at the early stages of humanity. Something very important has happened: man is no longer content to subsist by passively accepting only what his environment is able to offer him. Instead, he takes an active stand and discovers that floating with the stream is not necessarily the best option. He makes a transition from natural animal to cultural human.

We shall probably never be able to know for sure what caused that revolutionary change in the first place. From theological perspective, one can talk about a "divine spark" that was lit in the soul of the first man, endowing him with creative faculties. On the other hand, from anthropological perspective, we can perhaps say that nothing prevents us from viewing this "spark" as a necessary and logical outcome of preceding evolutionary trends. From that point of view, the discovery of creative initiative was perhaps no more "supernatural" than the other discovery that occurred billions of years before—when a few single-celled organisms suddenly "realized" that they could merge into a multi-cellular body by trading their independence for specialization within a more complex entity which was better suited for combatting external forces and ensuring survival.

Yet, as I have mentioned before, neither theology, nor anthropology is our concern in the present study. What is truly remarkable for a semiotician is the fact that the word which etymologically highlighted only the material aspect of this "rebellion against nature" is adopted to express the *spiritual* aspect of it as well. This was possible thanks to the perceived unity between the material and immaterial aspects of humanity in a situation when any technical innovation was also a spiritual one, i.e. always had a corresponding linguistic and religious effect.

It is time now, therefore, to define the two other essential components of culture—*language* and *technology*. Semiotically speaking, language can be characterized as *a system of signs used by human beings to communicate and interact with each other*. It is evident from this definition that language is a counterpart of religion in what they jointly constitute as *intellectual/ spiritual* (as opposed to material) *culture*. They are not the only components of this phenomenon but they are nevertheless essential to it. It is also important to stress that *communication* and *interaction* are defining attributes of both language and religion. That could mean that the "mechanism of action" that underlies both language and religion is largely identical. In the next two chapters where we shall speak about the origins of language and religion, I will try to show that this is actually the case.

As far as technology is concerned, it constitutes the spiritual/intellectual dimension of material culture, the *design* that accounts for all artefacts created by human beings. From semiotic perspective, technology can thus be defined as *a system of designations which mark the acquisition and use of specific objects in the specifically human way*. It is important to emphasize with regard to this definition that *designation* plays a crucial role in distinguishing a fact of nature from a fact of culture.

It is even more important once more to emphasize that various components of culture, although conventionally distinct, can be treated as phenomena of common origin which follow essentially the same "common law." This commonality is usually more evident and easier to trace at early stages of humanity but, as we shall see later, it remains identifiable even at very advanced stages. Therefore, throughout this book, we are going to consider religion in parallel with the other two crucial components of culture—technology and language—inasmuch as this simultaneity can be sustained without prejudice to the main subjects of our research—African Traditional Religion and Christianity.

What does it look like in practice—this primordial unity of technology, language and religion? I think the best way to understand it would be to study an example. Can we think of an object which is primarily used as a technological appliance but which at the same time can acquire certain properties that will allow us to consider it also as a religious and linguistic symbol? I believe such an object can be easily found in the history and even in the contemporary practice of mankind. It is well-known to all; it is a piece of wood that once broke off a tree and fell onto the ground, waiting for an insight of the primal inventor to put it to use. I am taking about the common wooden stick.

Its technological application is well-known. Although certain animals do use sticks for building their nests, dens or dams, their technology was not invented by them but by their *selfish genes* in order to assure a more efficient preservation of their species. The genes of higher primates were, on the other hand, mostly silent in that respect, leaving the initiative entirely to the individuals themselves. From the purely naturalistic point of view, a stick is nothing but a detached tree branch. It retains its "proper" use only as long as it remains attached to the tree—at the very best as something that can be gripped to facilitate climbing. A former branch lying on the ground is nothing but a useless obstacle which must be ignored or, at the very best, removed from the way. Yet, what used to signify an inconvenience suddenly changes its nature and begins to signify an opportunity to explore the potential of an object that initially seemed to be rejected by nature. Here we observe a process of "sign flipping," or, to use the biblical allusion that originally comes from the Psalms (118:22) and is repeated by Jesus (Matt 22:42, Mark 12:10, Luke 20:17)—*the stone rejected by builders becomes the head of the corner.*

However, this is just the beginning. Not only does man manage to reproduce and appropriate the experience of other species (birds, badgers or beavers), he also proceeds to discover further uses for the stick, which have no precedents among animals. From passive construction material the stick becomes an active extension of the human body. Depending on the specific application, it turns into a tool for digging or a weapon for fighting. Semiotically, it feels as if the same thing, without changing its shape or any other properties, acquires a new meaning, in a process similar to a word getting a *homonym*. This striking similarity suggests that the processes of acquiring technology and language (as well as religion) probably ran parallel, following the same basic rules, at least at the initial stage. We shall deal with language acquisition of little later. Right now, we can elaborate a bit on our example with the stick.

The above mentioned "homonymity" is not the only possible development. Another process which is probably even more important can, for lack of a better term, be designated as *metaphorization*.[1] To expound on our example with the stick, we can say that this time it is used not in an *alternative* but a in *figurative* sense, or, to put it differently, we can also say that it changes its sense from the technological to the communicative one. An *object* turns into a *symbol*, a stick becomes a staff, a rod, a scepter—whichever word will suit us to express its newly acquired quality as a sign of power and authority.

This "metaphoric" use of the stick most likely develops from its original use as a weapon. A *weapon* becomes a *symbol* as soon as it begins to signify that its owner can exercise the potential power inherent in that weapon at any time at his discretion, i.e. he can kill or injure anyone if he wishes to do so. As soon as this is realized by those around him, based on their previous experience, the actual physical use of the object becomes in most cases unnecessary. And when this realization becomes common currency among members of a certain social circle, the symbolical use of the object becomes the predominant one. There is no more need to strike anyone with the stick if it is enough simply to threaten with it to ensure obedience. Provided that this symbolical use remains generally accepted for a sufficiently long time, even threatening becomes unnecessary. It is now tacitly assumed that taking the stick and holding it in a conspicuous manner (usually upright) means that its possessor intends to issue an order which those he addresses are supposed to obey.

This is not the end of the development but probably the beginning of its most fascinating stage: the symbol becomes detached from its owner and acquires autonomous existence, while preserving its "moral" properties. In our example it is the power to assure obedience. The logic is simple: if the chief holds a stick in his hand in a special position every time when he gives an order, it can be concluded that no order can be given without that stick.

---

1. The role of metaphor as a "fundamental principle of man" was pointed out as early as 1873 by Nietzsche (in the article "On Truth and Falsity in their Ultramoral Sense" [Nietzsche, *Early Greek Philosophy & Other Essays*, 178]) who, however, later chose to replace it with "will to power"—an unfortunate move, in my opinion, because the latter is not unique to humans. Cassirer restores metaphor to this essential function, dedicating a whole chapter to it ("The Power of Metaphor") in his *Language and Myth* (1925). Both thinkers remain true to their philosophical idealism and approach the subject exclusively on psychological grounds, never even motioning technology (=material culture).

The power of authority is thus transferred from the person who originally commands it to the object originally used to express it. The symbol acquires *supernatural* properties. It becomes independent of its initial owner; it is now regarded as a moral tool or weapon that will work efficiently for anyone who will come in its possession. The scepter turns into a magic wand. Within our terminological system, this transformation can be called *metonymy*, i.e. when a transmission of sense occurs not through similarity of properties (as in the case of metaphor) but through the assumed association of two objects to each other.[2] From that point of view, magic is essentially nothing else but *metonymical use of a metaphorically transformed sign*.

---

2. Thus what J.G. Frazer in *The Golden Bough* (1889) calls "contagious magic" (Frazer, *The Golden Bough*, chapter 3, §3) precedes, in our opinion, what he calls "sympathetic magic."

Chapter II

The Origin of Language

WE SAW IN THE previous chapter that certain linguistic laws can be used to explain the genesis of some key elements of humanity, including material culture, thus revealing their common origin. However, it would all make sense only if these laws can also be applied to language itself. In other words, the question is: Does language obey the same laws as the other aspects of culture? Do these laws allow us to determine whether the symbolic forms of language can be derived from some pre-symbolic substratum, in line with the general pattern of deriving culture from nature?

The origin of language is a notoriously difficult subject. In the previous section we showed how a tool can be re-designated into a symbol of superhuman power. However, the same mechanism does not seem to apply to language to the same extent. Similar to the *stick*, language can be regarded as a tool initially supplied by nature, in the sense that in order to come into being it does not require to be "manufactured." Instead, it grows out of our certain bodily functions which originally have nothing to do with communication, like breathing or chewing.

The ability to utter sounds has evolved from *forced expiration* which meets a *deliberate* obstacle in the mouth, created through the use of our tongue, teeth and lips. This is a good example of using our respiratory tract in a modified (re-designated) way which is not unique to man but is shared with many other animals (remember also the non-exclusiveness of the use of the stick as construction material, as described in the previous section). Many animals, indeed, are able to produce sounds with communicative intent—mostly in order to deliver a threat or a warning to their congeners or sometimes to representatives of other species. However, animals express themselves predominantly in *signals*, not *symbols*. A specific set of signals makes a common possession of each species whose members inherit it in their genes, i.e. their signals are given to them by nature in the same way as certain survival skills are (ability to build nests, dens or dams etc.).

Humans also have some genetically inherited signals which, in similarity with those of animals, can be used to *attract attention* to something of which the meaning becomes evident *from context*. Thus, a shrill sound uttered by an animal or a human is usually intended primarily to make their neighbors aware of some trouble, inconvenience or deficiency which their responsive action can rectify. The specific nature of the predicament can in most cases be understood only if we know the circumstances that predetermine it. Thus, if someone blocks the passage of another individual, the sound signal (a shout in this case) to be given to the former will most likely impart a "give-way" message. Remarkably, this "animal" principle has been reproduced almost intact in the road traffic rules developed by humans in the twentieth century, where the sound signal (the horn) plays exactly the same supporting role as it usually does in the "traffic" of many higher mammals, while its exact meaning cannot be ascertained without knowledge of the situation that has provoked it.

However, unlike animals, humans can use not only a readily available set of signals but also creatively transform and recombine them (remember that we are talking about sound signals all this time) to make them into symbols. The main function of the symbol is to retain and communicate information the source of which is not immediately present. We cannot say that a symbol does not rely on context at all, but it is much less dependent on it and ideally seeks to overcome that dependence completely.

We do not know and will probably never know what gave the initial impetus to the rise of language, much in the same way as we do not know what initially gave rise to humanity in general. Perhaps the original function of language was very modest and secondary to that of "primal" signaling. Perhaps it was first used to transmit some supporting information while hunting in a team—information that was available to only one of the members who, for example, could be the only one to see the hunted animal. Most likely, it concerned identifying that animal ("It's a buffalo, not an antelope that I spot") or characterizing it in a certain way ("It's a large/small/wounded animal"). By receiving information about what they could not see by themselves, the other team members were better able to plan their further action.

As I have said above, a language symbol is formed by diversifying and recombining sounds originally given as a set of primal signals. Those signals, as we have seen, developed from the "metaphorical" use of certain physiological functions. A linguistic sign can therefore be described as a metaphor of a metaphor. As such, it signals an object that we discover as an obstacle in our way, both drawing our own attention to it and expressing the outcome of our interaction with it—getting it "out of our way." The best way to express such an interaction would be using at least three signals: that of the initial encounter (input), that of forming our attitude to the situation (processing) and that of our eventual response (output). Therefore, to operate a properly human language we would typically need symbols composed of at least three primal signals or, to put it in a more customary way, words of at least three sounds—two consonants and a vowel. This reinstates the once popular but nowadays often ridiculed idea that the first articulate words to be uttered by man were mostly monosyllabic. It should be emphasized, however, that "monosyllabic" does not mean "onomatopoeic." Onomatopoeic words are simply rudiments of the old *signaling* system that survives only as auxiliary part of human language. Articulate words, on the other hand, are built on completely different *symbolic* principles.

Thus, the *artificial* obstacle to the flow of air that we create in our mouth by pressing together our organs of speech in a certain combination constitutes an appropriate symbolic rendering of the *actual* obstacle we come across in the surrounding world when we see, hear or touch the object that occupies our attention. The choice of a particular symbolic "obstacle" (i.e. a linguistic sign) looks unmotivated for a modern observer, but it is difficult to tell how arbitrary it was for the primal speaker. Touching the teeth with the tongue may perhaps suggest the idea of greater "hardness" of the designated object than simply closing the lips which may imply greater "softness." It is quite possible that this designation was not initially arbitrary at all but represented the speaker's impressions from the few objects whose semiotic differentiation was of critical importance for the success of his enterprise (most likely, his hunting expeditions). It is also possible that when the circle of such essential objects started to get wider, all "new arrivals" into the vocabulary developed by analogy with the original pattern of distinctions.

The vowel that follows the initial consonant flows through the mouth is an unimpeded stream which is, however, subjected to a modulation of our choice selected from a very limited number of options (the number of vowels in most languages rarely exceeds ten) and as such provides an adequate representation of the free flow of thought in interpreting our encounter with an outside object.[1] It is difficult at the present stage of language development to tell whether the actual choice of that modulation—the quality and perhaps the quantity of the vowel sound—was originally arbitrary or determined (at least partially) by the emotional coloring associated with a particular sound. Traditionally, the /i/ sound is perceived, for example, as a "lighter" one than the /u/ sound which is commonly believed to suggest "darker," "gloomier" association, but it would be too hard to establish how universal that perception is in modern languages or was in the hypothetical protolanguage (*Ursprache*).

Finally, the consonant that concludes the hypothetical protoword represents our "response" to the encountered object, following its perception with our senses and realization of our impression expressed by the vowel. That processing results either in reproducing the same sound and thus acknowledging our "receipt" or uttering a different sound to emphasize our non-identity with the object. It is important to remember that the three sounds of the primordial word are originally mere signals emitted in the presence of the object. Yet these signals can be stored in memory and later reproduced in the absence of the object in order to signify it, i.e. to recall its presence when it is absent. This completes their transformation from signal to symbol, giving birth to human language.

It should be noted that the signals which merge into a word do not have to be three in number. Their number can be less, especially when they involve interaction with a fellow team member. In this case we may deal not with a "closed loop" of sense (input—processing—output) but with an open communicative impulse. This is why question particles are often only two-sound words and occasionally even single vowels. The latter can be regarded as original primitive signals that are directly converted into words or, alternatively, as words that have not completed their differentiation from signals, or perhaps even as words that reverted back to signals.

It is this sort of words that Giambattista Vico (1668–744) identifies as the most ancient monosyllabic units where the original nondescription of symbol and signal, word and sentence is still manifest. To illustrate the

---

1. Cf. the parallelism between the elemental structure of the world and the phonetic structure of the divine Word in Philo of Alexandria (c. 20 BC—c. 50 AD): "Naturally therefore will neither all earth be dissolved by all water which its bosom contains, nor will fire be extinguished by air, nor on the other hand will air be burnt up by fire, since the divine Word sets Himself as a boundary of the elements, like a vowel between consonants" . . . *Noah's Husbandry*, Bk. II, quoted by Eusebius of Caesarea (260/265–339/340) in *Preparation for the Gospel*, book. 7, chapter 13.

point, he quotes the imperative forms of a few basic Latin words in his *New Science*: *es, sta, i, da, dic, fac*: be, stand, go, give, say, do.[2]

Another good illustration of this point is provided by the famous Latin text, traditionally considered one of the possible shortest conversations, in terms of the number of sounds employed:

Quo is?—Eo rus—I![3]

It is worth going through that dialogue word by word, which should not take long anyway.

1. *Quo*—This is actually a two-sound word (the "qu" combination stands for one sound in classical Latin). It is a special word because its starting consonant corresponds to output, not input (as is usually the case with nouns). It is a signal that the speaker sends to his interlocutor in order to engage the latter's attention. The vowel that follows conventionally modulates the initial signal, specifying what sort of information the speaker queries for: to obtain a reference to the interlocutor's position / direction of movement. Obviously, there is no "input" component in this word which is "open-ended", an outgoing signal awaiting response. This is appropriately signified by the missing second consonant.

2. *Is*—This is an example of opposite nature—an input without output. The initial vowel expresses the speaker's passive perception of the interlocutor's action/intention. The "i" component in this case expresses to idea of perceived movement; the "s" component conventionally identifies the interlocutor as the person directly engaged in conversation (interaction) with the speaker.

3. *Eo*—A word consisting of vowels only, because it expresses the speaker's perception of himself—his own idea of movement and his own self-identification.

4. *Rus*—A typical three-sound word described above which uses the full tripartite pattern to express the speaker's interaction with it in the subject-to-object relationship.

5. *I*—Probably the most interesting part of the conversation, a sound which merges signal with symbol (see above) which (at least theoretically) can be used by both animal and man with the same meaning—to suggest that his fellow start moving. Under certain reservations, it can be interpreted it as a survivor from the primordial "language" of nature, dating from before the age of differentiation, irrespective of its actual history in Latin.

2. Giambattista Vico, *New Science*, location 3790.
3. Whither goest thou?—I go to the countryside.—Go!

The above example is, of course, exceptional. It would not be always that easy (if at all possible) to isolate protolanguage in other conversations, however short they may be. Certainly, the arbitrariness of linguistic sign increases with the development of culture in general. Yet, if the pattern outlined above is at least partially correct, it can serve a good illustration to the animal-to-human transformation we have observed in the example with technology—transformation which relies on the transition from "raw reality" to increasing degrees of its semiotic appropriation.

Chapter III

The Origin of Religion

Now that we have, to the best of our capabilities, navigated our way through the difficult question of the origin of language, it will be much easier to answer the same question about religion, for, as I have noted above, language and religion (as well as technology) share a common origin and function in many respects in the same way. To see how it can be possible, we must advance a step further in our understanding of the mechanism of signification.

We have noted above that the linguistic sign (or, indeed, any other symbol) allows us to store an object in our memory in order to reproduce it later in communication. Of course, we do not mean to say that our brain stores a physical object; neither do we mean a graphical image of that object (a kind of photocopy) which gets imprinted in our mind. Communication with pictures has only a limited value and circulation among mankind. Rather, we mean storing mental images which originally might have reflected our sensual interaction with their counterparts in the external world through raising and combining signals in our mind, but which later evolved into conventional links between outward things and their mental correlates that did not resemble each other in appearance anymore. To put it more concisely, during verbal intercourse we invoke the *ideas* of objects, not the objects themselves.

Whether that idea (demon/spirit/soul) has an existence independent of our mind or whether it exists only in our imagination is not the semiotician's concern. The question belongs to the domain of philosophy or theology. The actual answers given to it by various thinkers at various times often contradict each other. Even if we had a conclusive answer to that question, it would change nothing in our approach of *thinking of signs in signs*. For the purposes of this study it is enough to point out that, whether truly existent or not, the idea is always treated by man *as if* its existence were an indisputable fact. This is because we invariably rely on that existence by invoking it in our communication. This essential rule has never changed over the whole history of mankind, and from that point of view, there is essentially no difference between an early Paleolithic and an early twenty-first century man in the way they assume the reality of ideas. Without the belief in that reality human communication (and by extension, culture) would collapse. Even if someone tried to deny the objective existence of ideas, he would still have to rely on language to express his denial and by doing so have to appeal to their assumed reality. He would thus get into a vicious circle which we are going to consider in some more detail when it comes to discussing atheism in chapter XI.

What does it all have to do with religion? Well, nearly everything because the only difference between language and religion is that the former invokes the idea of a thing during interhuman communication, while the latter does so during human interaction with the thing itself. The discovery/invention of language creates a double perception of every single object man has to deal with: its "direct" material meaning conveyed by the senses and its "figurative" ideal meaning manifested in the symbol. As we have shown above, initially the thing and its symbol exist in organic unity—one grows from the other, the object determines its own signification. As time passes, this link becomes more and more strained but always endures to the end.

Therefore, in the primitive state of affairs, any contact with any material object, any use of it or any attempt to change it inevitably involves a contact with, a use of, or a change in the symbol (demon/soul/idea) of that object at the same time. In the animistic worldview, any object, as soon it acquires a name, automatically receives a soul too. Conversely, the sum of the souls of the objects known to us by name constitutes both our language and our original "pantheon." The only difference is, once again, that we refer to a specific demon of a specific thing when we want to pass information about it to our fellow human being (in which case it is language) and we address that demon directly when we want to do something to that thing or want that thing to do something for us (in which case it is religion). Obviously, we should never forget that this primordial unity always involves technology as well, which at this stage of human evolution cannot be separated from religion. Thus, the utterance addressed to the tree which is about to supply man with his first manufactured tool—"O Tree! Let me make a stick out of thee!"—is a spell aimed at the spirit of the tree to be *sacrificed* and an expression of technical design at the same time, i.e. a piece of technology, language and religion simultaneously.

This original unity of spirit and matter commonly known as "animism" makes up a significant component of all religions, even though none has preserved it intact (we shall see why it is the case when we talk about the Fall of Man). Under this traditional system, any material object and its ideal counterpart (its name/soul/demon) exist in perfect togetherness and unobstructed reciprocity of signification. Every known object of the phenomenal world has a correspondence in the noumenal one; everything is sacred, nothing is prophane; the universe presents a universal hierophany. Every piece of information is revelation, every walk a procession, every act a ritual, every phrase a spell. What is also important to note is that every member of society at this stage has equal access to this animistic pool. There are no "more inspired" or "less inspired people"; revelation is equally available to everyone; there is no distinction between laity and priesthood.

In modern society, it is a common belief (first introduced by European Romantics in the early nineteenth century) that the child's mind is the most common approximation of what previously could be enjoyed by everyone:

> There was a time when meadow, grove, and stream,
> The earth, and every common sight,
> To me did seem
> Apparelled in celestial light,
> The glory and the freshness of a dream.
> It is not now as it hath been of yore;—
> Turn wheresoe'er I may,
> By night or day.
> The things which I have seen I now can see no more.

These introductory lines of the "Ode: Intimations of Immortality from Recollections of Early Childhood"[1] by William Wordsworth (1770–1850) contain both glorification of primordial spirituality and lamentation of its subsequent loss. Such a loss, however, is inevitable for reasons we are going to discuss in the next chapter.

---

1. The same lines are quoted by Tylor in *Primitive Culture*, vol. 2, chapter XII, as a perfect illustration of animistic perception of reality. The first use of the very word "animism" is also credited to this author.

Chapter IV

The Fall of Man

THE IDYLLIC UNITY BETWEEN matter and spirit, body and soul, thing and its name, tool and religious symbol cannot last forever. Arbitrariness creeps into this semiotic paradise at the same time as the treacherous Serpent slithers into the Garden of Eden. The more artefacts spring up around, the more difficult it becomes to control their spiritual counterparts. Yet, it is still deemed to be possible by grouping them around those things that are supposed to be "given by nature" (despite the fact that they, as we remember, are only products of culture). The names of such things seem to have accompanied them from the very beginning, or—more precisely—to have grown out of man's mastering their usage through daily interaction with them (see chapter II).

However, as technology grows more and more sophisticated, it becomes more and more difficult to map new artefacts to their natural "equivalents" and to establish their semiotic correspondences. As the number of artefacts starts to grow exponentially, this process spirals out of control. New names have thus to be invented rather than inferred, in the same way as new tools and appliances can no longer be traced to their natural "precedents." But invention is something that proceeds entirely from man, something that nature (=God) has been unable or unwilling to supply in the first place. In a sense, inventing a thing (a piece of technology, a symbol) looks like going against the will of God whom man tries to outsmart or even disobey in appropriating things not designed for him. This feeling of countering the will of God has deeply imprinted itself into the collective memory of mankind as recollection of an inexpiable sin committed by man at the very beginning of his career. In the prevailing Christian idiom of the last couple of millennia this perceived transgression has been commonly known as the Fall of Man.

The biblical account of this incident is, however, far from unique. The story of man's falling out with God is present in nearly all world religions and mythologies.[1] It is certainly well represented in Africa too. Thus, according to the well-known Akan version of the myth, the original conflict between divinity and humanity was provoked by a woman who was too zealous in working with a pestle which she was using to pound cereal mash—an essential operation in preparing *fufu*, a staple of West African cuisine. It is usually told that while doing so she was disrespectfully hitting the deity, who finally took offense and decided to withdraw from the world he had created.

The story may look strange to a modern reader. Why did God choose to locate himself so close to that woman? Why could he not move only a little bit upwards or aside to stay out of reach of the annoying pestle? It seems that he was annoyed not so much by physical contact as by the fact that a human being was using a *tool*. It was the *artefact* that irritated the Deity—something the use of which he did not know himself, something that man had invented independently, something that had not been given to man by nature. It is God, not the woman, who seems to initiate the conflict in this story, who deliberately approaches her as close as possible in order to expose himself to her blows. He probably felt annoyed as soon as he saw the woman start her operations.

Another important aspect of this story is the fact that the woman was busy preparing a meal from something that was ultimately a product of cultivation. As we have already pointed out, agriculture is a relatively late occurrence in history, which tends to monopolize the idea of culture in general and thus cause some confusion in terms. It also means that the myth in question dates from the same stage of society as the Hebrew myth—the age of transition from hunter-gathering to land cultivation. Whatever the dating, God's response to the situation is quite typical and can equally be applied to any stage of culture. By his withdrawal from the terrestrial world, he wants to show that "man doth not live by bread only" (Deuteronomy 8:3), i.e. must not rely entirely on agriculture/technology. Technology causes a rift between man and God, as the artefacts it creates keep causing ever greater disobedience and miscommunication. This alienation must be cured if man cares for his salvation.

---

1. A representative, though far from complete, selection of relevant stories from world mythologies can be found in Frazer's *Folk-lore in the Old Testament* (1918), chapter II.

The Hebrew version of this myth highlights another important aspect which makes it especially valuable for our study. According to the Book of Genesis (chapter 3) it was man's tasting the forbidden fruit that provoked God's anger and caused their subsequent separation. We leave aside the agricultural aspect of the incident because we do not know what kind of fruit was under divine prohibition. Perhaps it was the first product of pomiculture, the first tree grown from seed, but there is no way for us to find it out. Let us rather concentrate on the effect of consuming that fruit: "And the eyes of them both were opened, and they knew that they *were* naked" (Gen 3:7). What does this discovery mean from semiotic perspective? Quite a lot.

To start with, realizing one's own nudity is a very cultural fact, as nudity in the cultural sense means something very different from nudity in the purely physical sense. To eliminate nudity culturally, it is enough to cover not the whole body but only a small part of it—one's genitals. This is obviously what Adam and Eve do in Genesis which says that they made themselves "aprons." But why the genitals and not any other part of the body? Different explanations are possible, but we shall here concentrate on the semiotic ones. It can be simply because the genitals are located in the geometric center of the body and thus considered the most important parts due to their position. However, one can also venture a more sophisticated guess. Genitals are strongly associated with *tools* (in fact we can "reversely" apply this interpretation to the Akan myth too—because of the obvious associative connection between "pestle" and "penis"). Of course, these tools are "God-given" and as such cannot be viewed as cultural artefacts. Yet it is possible to read the myth as a story of originally natural tools for which a symbolic use is discovered.

Such a "discovery," of course, is only possible after man has become familiar with other, proper, tools—first of all, the stick. The suddenly revealed resemblance between man's sexual organ and one of his most essential tools allows him to *metaphorize* the former as something that at least partially belongs to the realm of technology and not only physiology. But we also remember that at the early stages of culture any tool is also a magical symbol (the erect penis is certainly a symbol of authority of man over woman—leaving aside the later religious roles of the phallus). A magical symbol incorporated into the human body requires special attention, which is promptly manifested by covering it. Thus, a cover on human genitals becomes a sign of man's belonging to culture and his alienation from nature. Alienation in this case is synonymous with disobedience to God.

To take an example of a less intimate character, a mere technological one, let us see what sort of taboo is still rigorously observed by those who inhabit the shores of Lake Busumtwi[2] in the Ashanti Region, Ghana. Specifically, there is a strict prohibition on using any vessels to sail that lake for the purpose of fishing, apart from very primitive planks or rafts. The reason is that the said lake is a sacred one. But how can the use of, say, a more sophisticated rowing boat desecrate it? The answer will be obvious after what we have known about the religious significance of technology: the use of a plainly recognizable artefact would offend the deity of that lake, much in the same fashion as the use of a pestle offends the Supreme Being in the previously cited myth. Only "natural vessels" are therefore permitted.

A similar reason lies behind the prohibition to cross the lake from one shore to another. The lake is round in shape and crossing it along the diameter line would mean to cross out the divine circle, to prove the finitude of an infinite figure, in short, to offend the deity in a symbolic way again. Neither taboo seems to have any immediate economic expedience; on the contrary, they create artificial obstacles (demand some "sacrifice") to prevent alienation with the local deity, to insure his protection and assistance in any fishing enterprise.

Although, as we saw from previous examples, man's disobedience to God's command can be viewed from semiotic perspective as a necessary condition of overcoming animality and acquiring humanity, the first steps in that direction are taken with extreme caution. All efforts are made to downplay man's initiative in committing this critical trespass. Almost in all cases there is also a third party involved which is supposed to bear at least part of the blame. It is often some animal, most likely a *totem*, a liaison agent between man and nature, that instigates the original deviation from divine rules. Very often that animal is expected to act as a mere messenger of God, but it nearly always, either accidentally or deliberately, distorts the message or fails to deliver it. As a consequence, it is apportioned its own part of divine punishment. The biblical Serpent certainly fits into that category.[3]

Gradually, the zoomorphic totem yields to the anthropomorphic one—the so called "culture hero." The latter usually has free access to the realm of spirits but often abuses the trust of the Supreme Being. His motives are at first rather egoistic—he is often a *trickster* who wants to cheat the gods to his own advantage, but his tricks ultimately turn to the benefit of mankind. He often partially preserves his zoomorphism which he swaps for human shape whenever he finds it convenient. The Akan mythology has a

---

2. I follow the Wikipedia spelling of this name. Both the Bradt Guide and Rattray spell it as "Bosomtwe" (see *Ashanti*, pp. 54–76). I also have first-hand experience of observing those sacred planks in use by fishermen, although not of personal involvement in their use.

3. See the already quoted chapter from Frazer.

perfect example of such a trickster-hero—the great Anansi, an archetypal spider-man who manages to prove his supremacy among the other animals to the Supreme Being (Nyame) but who also teaches the humans one of their staple crafts—that of weaving, the secret of which he at some point certainly stole from the gods.

In extreme examples, the culture hero may completely part with his trickster status and even sacrifice his wellbeing for the sake of mankind. Such is the famous figure of Greek mythology—Prometheus—who in order to assure the earthly inhabitants' transition from animality to humanity is prepared to incur the divine wrath of Zeus, the supreme sky god, who, in spite of his own totemic past, has now conceitedly installed himself on Mount Olympus and cares little for the troubles of ordinary people. In fact, however, there was nothing to steal: technology, as we remember, was a purely human initiative. The culture hero is nothing but a "cover-up story" thought out later in order to transfer (at least partially) the blame of culture from the human to the divine realm.

This downplay of human guilt, with or without the help of a totemic hero, initially succeeds in its goal—to make the shift to culture pass unnoticed. The first tools used by man (sticks and stones) have no outward distinction from nature-given objects. The divine prohibition of human initiative—the famous taboo imposed on Adam and Eve—looks hardly broken. To draw a parallel with language, we can say that the first pieces of technology (which double as religious signs) look more like inherited signals, still about to be rethought and recombined as symbols. In their early shape, they pass for "imitation of nature" allowing man (up to a certain limit, of course) to stay disguised as an innocent citizen of the animal kingdom. Yet, the very ability to use them alternately as technological tools and magical objects betrays the actual loss of innocence. A common stick can be used just as efficiently for digging as it can be employed, e.g., for divination.

The latter use, by the way, has been preserved intact in some parts of Africa. I personally observed such divination sessions at a market in Kara, Northern Togo, where the diviner and his client would grab the same rough stick and poke it randomly at spots which their synergy would determine (see figure 1 below). Perhaps originally that technique had more applications than it does today. Perhaps in the past it could be also used, e.g., to identify the spot to dig a waterhole or lay the foundation of a new building. But perhaps I am simply unaware of such uses only due to the gaps in my knowledge of Africa.

Figure 1. Stick divination in Togo

Another essential tool/weapon of mankind—the stone—shows a similar differentiated application. At first, only raw unhewn stones are used for digging / fighting / scraping animal skins as technology and, as a religious parallel to that, for building altars. Exodus 20:25 makes it perfectly explicit when YHWH says to Moses, "And if thou wilt make me an altar of stone, thou shalt not build it of hewn stone: for if thou lift up thy tool upon it, thou hast polluted it." The reason behind this command is obvious: stones dedicated to God must be made by God himself. To apply any tool to nature originally means to pollute it. Even when the obvious advantage of "improving" nature is discovered, efforts are made to find such objects that would look like products of technology but would be of natural origin at the same time. Hence the value attached to regularly shaped pieces used for that purpose. Here is an example from Sir Edward Burnett Tylor (1832-1917):

> It is remarkable to what late times full and genuine stone-worship has survived in Europe. In certain mountain districts of Norway, up to the end of the last century, the peasants used to preserve *round stones*, washed them every Thursday evening (which seems to show some connection with Thor), smeared them with butter before the fire, laid them in the seat of honor on fresh straw, and at certain times of the year steeped them in ale, that they might bring luck and comfort to the house.[4]

4. *Primitive Culture*, vol II, chapter XIV, emphasis added. Tylor's own source is Nilsson, *Primitive Inhabitants of Scandinavia*, 241.

It is no less remarkable in the above example what a strenuous effort is put forth to humanize and domesticate this "natural artefact." Butter, ale and even straw are all products of cultivation and at first sight may seem to "pollute" the symbol which is perceived as originating from the thunder-god himself. Yet in this case the effect is opposite. The "divine" object is apparently expected to purify and sanctify the base substances among which it is placed. Here we have an attempt to reconcile culture with nature on the strength of outward resemblance.

We do not know what shape were the twelve stones that Joshua ordered to pluck out of the dry riverbed of the Jordan while the Jewish tribes under his command were crossing it (Josh 4:1–15). It is very likely they were smooth and polished by constant contact with flowing water and therefore looked quite *round*. We do not know either how those stones were treated in Gilgal at "the place where they lodged" but it is just as likely that they would make up fireplace (such hearths are still common in many parts of Africa, e.g., in the Northern Region of Ghana). This way they could be used both as a stove and as an altar, i.e. both for technological and religious purposes (cooking and sacrifice).

Here is another example from my "fieldwork." While in Togo, this time in its central part, I visited a shrine maintained by a Voodoo priest. Characteristically for West Africa, it featured many different deities, some of them even in conflict with each other. They seemed, nevertheless, to enjoy equal rights, each having his or her own altar, some inside, some outside the modest hut[5] which served as their common temple. What especially fascinated me was the structure erected to represent Gu, the famous West African iron god (better known by his Yoruba name, Ogun). It was completely built of various scrap metal pieces, mostly discarded motorcycle parts, as far as I could deduce. One would expect that a god who specially patronizes makers of artefacts (blacksmiths etc.) should have some custom-made artefact for his symbol. Yet the author of the altar chose to go for an object "not made by hands." It did not matter that the parts used for that structure had originally been manufactured by humans. Once such things are discarded at large, they cease to be proper artefacts, they revert—in a way—to the lap of nature, where they become purified and sanctified by the god. They thus acquire the same status as the Norwegian round stones—things divine in their nature which only resemble human artefacts and can therefore serve as religious symbols.

Symbols not made by hands, the so called *acheiropoietic* images, are also valued in Christianity. The Image of Edessa, the Shroud of Turin, and

---

5. See also Case Study 2.

the Veil of Veronica are probably the best-known examples. Similar images are venerated in many other religions. As we have seen, their original function is to conceal or at least to soften the Fall of Man, to portray it as something where non-human forces are implicated. Such "non-human artefacts" are presented as material evidence that demonstrates direct involvement of nature or at least participation of some intermediary semidivine actor in their creation. However, such symbols, due to their borderline position, sooner or later start to be regarded as dubious and finally tend to be rejected as they are defenseless against the reproach that by using them for religious purposes we worship the creature instead of the creator. Such a treatment will make no difference between paying homage to the sun or other heavenly bodies and "bowing to stick and stone." Sooner or later, these "natural" symbols have to give way to purely artificial ones, much in the same way as "natural" sounds give way to articulate words in the development of language. In the realm of religion these manmade images are commonly known as *fetishes* and *idols*.

Chapter V

Reclaiming the Fetish

DESPITE ALL THE TERMINOLOGICAL controversy that surrounds the use of the word "fetish," I believe that nobody has so far come up with a better term that denotes a very important part of any religion—its visual symbolism. I therefore insist on using it throughout this book. In doing so, I am allied with "common people," including traditional practitioners themselves, who almost invariably stick to the word "fetish," most likely because they intuitively find it appropriate. Viewed semiotically, fetishes exist in virtually all world religions, not only those which are commonly defined as "traditional" (or sometimes "primal"). It seems, however, that many spokesmen of global monotheistic religions still lack goodwill (or perhaps even courage) to acknowledge that existence.

So, for the purpose of this study, we define "fetish" as *an artefact that provides ideoplastic representation of a certain spiritual object*. The key words in this definition are "artefact" and "ideoplastic." The first one follows the etymology: "fetish" derives from the Portuguese *feitiço* which in its own turn is a reflex of the Latin *facticius* "made by art." As in the previously studied example with "culture," the etymology in this case also proceeds from the "material" meaning which is subsequently extended into the spiritual domain. So, originally, "fetish" means any piece of technology that results in the creation of an artefact that does not (unlike the idol/icon) directly imitate the external appearance of any natural object. Hence the second key word—"ideoplastic"—which means "employed for expressing a certain idea through material (3D) shapes." These shapes constitute a set of expressive means (signs) which, similarly to linguistic signs (phonemes), can be combined in a certain conventional manner to form socially recognizable semiotic entities.

A word can therefore be metaphorically defined as a spoken fetish; a fetish, on the other hand, can be characterized as a sculptured word. A written word can then be construed as a two-dimensional variety of fetish, especially if it is written using an ideographic system (as in Chinese, but not a hieroglyphic system as in Ancient Egyptian which is closer to the idol/icon as a means of expression). However, even the alphabetic script fits this definition just as well. We are going to discuss later what consequences this statement involves for the monotheistic denial of the fetish.

Right now we can point out that, similarly to what we have suggested for language, the ideoplastic means of expression originally employed for the fetish were *not arbitrary*. Just in the same way as consonantal and vocal sounds could have initially represented certain sensory encounters experienced during man's interaction with his environment, so certain straight or curved lines, round or angular shapes, smooth or rough surfaces etc. could have stood for specific physical perceptions metaphorized into mental conceptions. Also in a similar way, with the expansion of the circle of ideas to be denoted by language, this non-arbitrary convention could have later broken down and given way to an arbitrary one, which resulted in the inability for the fetish maker to explain why his product had a certain shape and not any other one.

However, with many ideoplastic signs (fetishes) the original correspondence between the sensory impression and figural expression can be easier to trace than for linguistic (verbal) signs. To justify this claim, let us first examine the fetish which I bought at the Akodessawa Market in Lomé and still have in my possession. I do not know its name—perhaps my Togolese friends or specialists, if they chance upon this book, will be able to recognize and identify it after reading the description and looking at the photograph below.

Case Study 3. The Fetish of the Akodessawa Market

The fetish is quite tiny in size—the length of less than two phalanges of my index finger (see figure 2 below). It consists of two roughly hewn pieces of wood (which species—I am, once again, unable to tell): the larger and the smaller one. The larger one is cylindrical in shape, with two blunt ends/butts, one of them markedly wider than the other. The wider butt is cut out in such a way as to narrow down towards the middle of the stick whose "waist" is thus clearly marked. There is a hole drilled in the wider butt, quite close to the middle line. The hole does not go through the full width of the stick but stops approximately halfway through. Viewed with the wider end pointing downwards, the piece resembles a woman wearing a long skirt; the hole, in that case, can be associated with the anus or vagina. Viewed with the wider end pointing upwards, it looks like a homunculus with a flat-top head. The hole in that case resembles an open mouth.

The smaller part is a thin pin, the length of my little finger's top phalanx, sharpened at one end and blunt at the other. It is tied to the larger piece by means of twisted wire whose material (as one can now easily expect) I cannot identify. Most of that wire is wound around the narrower butt of the main piece—four turns altogether. The winding is done is such a way as to prevent the wire from slipping off the butt—apparently the manufacturer's knowhow. One strand of the wire branches from the second loop at the middle and thus forms a loose end, looking very much like the homunculus' arm. The sharpened pin (the smaller bit) is attached to the end of it in the same trademark non-slip-off manner. The sharp end of the pin can be inserted into the hole of the larger part or let loose at the owner's will. The whole assembly, depending on the orientation of the larger bit and insertion/withdrawal of the smaller one, evokes the following associations:

- With the wider butt pointing upwards and pin let loose, it resembles a man about to help himself to a banana
- With the wider butt pointing upwards and pin inserted, it looks more like a man smoking a cigar or blowing a bugle
- With the wider butt pointing downwards and pin let loose, it looks like a man who has just unsheathed his sword and has drawn his arm back, about to lunge at his adversary
- With the wider butt pointing downwards and pin inserter, it resembles a man (or a woman) administering himself an enema or perhaps masturbating

Figure 2. The Fetish of the Akodessawa Market

The market trader who sold me the fetish said that its principal use was to bring good luck to travelers. I think, however, that he mentioned only one of many possible uses which he found most relevant for my situation, based on the assumption that all tourists are travelers and, therefore, in need of an appropriate travel-facilitating device. I believe that the actual number of possible applications is significantly greater, judging by the large variety of associations evoked by the fetish. Yet I also think that all those numerous applications can be arranged into two essential categories which can be conventionally styled as "mission about to be taken" and "mission accomplished."

Thus, the braid on the slim end inevitably suggests the idea of a bond which, in turn, suggests the idea of power trammeled and due about to be released, stored energy about to be converted into motion, a swing of the arm about to deal a blow etc. The loose strand of the same bond suggests, on the other hand, the idea of liberation and movement. In that case, the braid looks like imparting its momentum to the pin whose sharp end is in binary opposition to the blunt butts, counterpoising action and rest, deliberation and decision. The owner of the fetish can repeatedly insert and withdraw the pin in a series of unconscious movements repeated an indefinite number of times—the more repetitions the better, the greater the number of assertive actions, going on and on like a silent mantra. In and out, crank and shaft, systole and diastole, conception and delivery, strain and relaxation, reveille and curfew, war and diplomacy etc. etc.—the list can be continued *ad infinitum*. The little fetish embodies the eternal wisdom of "dared and done." It is a symbol that inspires self-reliance but also a tool that assures "plugging" into the iterative cycle of the universe, a device that synchronizes the owner with a phase of cosmic waves which will eventually carry him to success and prosperity. This tiny artefact is worth volumes of blabber about "positive thinking" and "learning from nature."

We can also add that its universal appeal and applicability make it look quite *monotheistic* in its design. Even though it may originally have been linked to some polytheistic deity (of which I am not sure and therefore invite experts to share their knowledge of the subject) it has long since shed its parochial appearance and entered the public domain.

Chapter VI

Rethinking the Idol

We define "idol" as *imitative representation of a spiritual entity*. Such representation is usually three-dimensional (3D). Two-dimensional (2D) representation is usually referred to as "icon." Idols generally precede icons in the history of religion because 2D representation demands a greater level of abstraction. However, all that we are going to say about idols also applies to icons. The umbrella term for both types of representation would be "visual image." However, in the rest of this chapter we prefer to use "idol" as a generic term because of its obvious associations with traditional religions.

As imitative representation, the idol is different from the fetish whose type of representation is *ideoplastic*, in the sense that the former does not imitate the appearance of the object it represents. This means that the semiotic mechanisms of fetish and idol are very different, even though their practical applications in religion are often identical. Thus, unlike the fetish that "does not care for appearances," the idol aims at visual representation (with varying degrees of typification vs individualization) of something that already exists in the material world. In this sense, it imitates nature. In this capacity, the idol has its linguistic correspondence in onomatopoeic words—signs that reproduce (imitate) sounds already available in nature which are re-appropriated as symbols at the service of man.

It is in the secondary, symbolic, quality that both idol and onomatopoeia can be used—with fetishes and words being their ideographic counterparts—as signs that point to a transcendental spiritual entity (soul/demon/deity). That entity is at first inseparably connected with its signifier but can subsequently acquire greater freedom and evolve towards developing an arbitrary association. Thus an animal figure carved out of wood (just as an onomatopoeic word that originally presented the sound emitted by that animal) can be adopted to express not only the general idea of that animal but also (through metonymic narrowing) a generic quality of that animal (e.g., courage for the lion, keen eyesight for the eagle etc.). In short, imitation becomes ideation. The image no longer points to an object from the material world but to its spiritual attribute in the world of ideas. An animal or, even more so, a human figure are obvious candidates for expressing the idea of an *intelligent being* and, by extrapolation, of *intelligent design*. In fact, this is the preferred way for symbolical depiction of intelligence nearly in all primal religions most of whose visual images are either zoomorphic or anthropomorphic.

It is worth noting that idols in religion often play a much more important role than onomatopoeic words in language. This is because visual information can be easily stored on analogue media (pictures and statues = icons and idols) while audial information, until fairly recently, could be stored only in human memory or in graphic form, i.e. as writing and that only in those cultures that had it at their disposal. On the other hand, some religions go without idols, while there are probably no languages that can do without onomatopoeia, even though its role in most of them is very limited. This is very different with fetishes without which, as we pointed out in the previous chapter, no religion can do, just as no language can do without proper words.

Both idol and fetish constitute a step forward on the way of man's increasing control over nature and improvement of his semiotic assets. As such, they enjoy great popularity among traditional religions. Yet, just like the "natural" symbols which we discussed in chapter IV, they inevitably come to be perceived as inadequate. This is because their conflicting properties become evident and, sooner or later raise the following question: How can a finite object (image) express something which is infinite by definition (deity)? This contradiction is less painfully felt by polytheistic religions than by monotheistic ones. Nevertheless, all religions that have developed the idea of the Supreme Being face this impasse one way or another.

The most common solution offered for this problem is to limit the means of signification employed for the Supreme Being, both pictographic and ideographic ones (i.e. idols and fetishes). In the extreme-case scenario, the Supreme Being can be denied all signification completely (see chapter X). In practice, however, most religions want to avoid a situation when the cognition of God is impossible by any means other than mystical ones. While idolatry, as we have noted, can be given up completely (in the same way as all onomatopoeic words can be, theoretically, expelled from any language), some fetishism, i.e. ideographic representation of deity, has to be allowed. In fact, it can often happen that the more iconoclastic a religion tries to be, the more pronounced can be the role of fetishism in it.

In Judaism, for example, the means of expressing the idea of God are reduced to a drastic minimum. The only legitimate way of doing so is to use the four-character word (Tetragrammaton) which is allowed in its written version only, while its spoken version is tabooed. As a result, the role of graphic representation becomes more important in Judaism than in any other religion. The written word takes absolute priority over the spoken one. The consequences of this semiotic imbalance are multifarious and, in no small part, are accountable for the rise of Christianity when other conditions become ripe at a certain point in history. We shall discuss this event in detail in chapter XIII.

However, the Tetragrammaton is not the only occurrence of "fetishism" in Judaism. Another object which can be considered to have acquired obvious features of a fetish is the Jerusalem Temple. We remember from Case Study 2 that YHWH had no permanent abode from the time he first appeared to Moses until the age of King David, i.e. long after the Jews became a sedentary people. When the idea to build a permanent residence first came to the king's mind, it provoked a controversy and an eloquent protest from the prophet Nathan which ultimately lead to indefinite suspension of the project. That controversy seems to originate not so much from the fact that God reserved the implementation of that idea for David's successor but from the uneasy feeling that many had about erecting an immovable structure, an *artefact* that could be easily identified with God himself. Such identification would mean "fetishism" for many adepts of Judaism. For them, the temporary abode (the Tabernacle) with which God had until then contented himself, looked, quite paradoxically, more adequate than the fixed one conceived by David. A temporary movable structure may be thought to serve the purpose better because it is not attached to any fixed spot. It could thus be better at expressing the idea of God's omnipresence.

When we turn to the New Testament, we find Jesus in full acceptance of the perfect semiotic identity between God and His domicile (the Temple), whether "artificial" or the "natural" one, as evidenced in the Gospel of Matthew (Mt 8:20):

> And whoso shall swear by the temple, sweareth by it, and by him that dwelleth therein. And he that shall swear by heaven, sweareth by the throne of God, and by him that sitteth thereon.

Claiming anything to the contrary is, according to Jesus, sheer hypocrisy. As such, this statement constitutes an admission of impossibility to go completely fetish-free. We should not be therefore surprised when John the Divine makes the next step in this direction and identifies the Temple with Christ's own body (John 2:21) in line with the elated theology promoted by the fourth gospel but also in continuation of the same evolutionary trend of symbolic representation. What could stand for the Father can is just as well stand for the Son.

By acting as a living temple Jesus (although only for a short while) overcomes the inadequacy of divine representation by human means, as his body is believed both to *contain* and to *reveal* God at the same time. The rift between humanity and divinity (see chapter IV) is thus repaired but only as long as Christ maintains his bodily presence on earth. This fulness of this presence is badly compromised by his trial and execution. Being nailed/bound to the cross, his body is deprived of movement and thus literally "idolized." It is remarkable that it is in this immobile state that his later followers have preferred to depict him, instead of, as it might seem more appropriate, his mobile states before Crucifixion or after Resurrection. This is mostly due to three reasons: a) the attraction of any borderline/transitional state between life and death; b) the relative easiness of presenting static states compared to dynamic ones; and c) the importance of depicting Jesus in line with the "Man of Sorrows" tradition. The implications of the last item for Africa will be briefly discussed in chapter XVI.

In the later centuries of Christianity, the crucifix as an image undergoes further evolution in presentation. The body vanishes from the cross and the idol becomes a fetish—to be reproduced and multiplied in greatest numbers as the chief symbol of that religion. This is not surprising either: the obvious advantage that the cross has over the crucifix is the higher diversity of meanings. The cross can act not only as a sign of God's voluntary suffering but also in a more traditional role—as a symbol of divine power spreading in all directions etc.

Some Christian denominations are more aware than others about the fetishist implications of that symbolism. For that reason, they avoid using the crucifix and even the plain cross in their religious services or on their paraphernalia. Yet, as we have noted above, it is impossible to eliminate graphic representation (fetishes) completely. Certainly for believers, God's very name, as soon as it is written, printed, or pronounced in any language, immediately acquires supernatural properties through reference to its divine signified. Next comes the Bible as a physical object, especially in the Protestant branches of Christianity, where it is a symbol of choice (because other "sacred" objects tend to be discredited as "fetishes"). Similarly to the

Temple which both contains and represents God, this book both is supposed to contain and denote his Word as a whole. Swearing on the Bible looks, therefore, just as appropriate as swearing by the Temple, the legitimacy of which was so passionately defended by Jesus himself.

Chapter VII

Blood as Spiritual Currency

IN THE PREVIOUS CHAPTER, speaking about the body of Christ, we mentioned that it simultaneously reveals and constitutes a divine substance. Any Christian would, however, say to it that this characterization is incomplete unless we add another important substance—*blood*. Both flesh and blood act in this case as symbolic substances or it would be just as correct to say, *spiritual substances*. Both flesh and blood, viewed this way, have a material and a spiritual value, by constituting and at the same time revealing the supernatural essence that they represent. Yet, although they may equally point to the same signified, they do not always relate to each other as completely parallel signifiers. Rather, their interrelationship can be that of *gradation*. Blood, due to its *liquid* nature, can be perceived to have a higher degree of spirituality than *solid* flesh, even though this spiritual superiority has never been formally recognized in Christianity. However, in most ancient traditions, the blood acts as the body's spiritual "filler," something that endows it with vital force. This gradational distinction of blood is clearly evidenced in the Book of Leviticus which states that "the life of the flesh is in the blood" (17:11). This is why in the same book blood is deemed to be inappropriate for human consumption.

However, even blood does not belong to the highest degree on this scale of spiritualization. There is still a higher instance above it—that of *breath/wind* which, in the same ancient tradition, is often identified with *soul/deity* itself. Its more tenuous (gaseous) nature makes this perception all the more obvious. At the same time, its residual materiality allows it to retain the same double function as both a constituent and a designatory medium. This is clearly evidenced in the famous passage from the Gospel of John (3:8) which in the original Greek says *"To pneuma hopou thelei pnei"* and which can be translated into English as either "The wind bloweth where it listeth" (as in the King James Version) or as "The Spirit breatheth where he will" (as, for example, in the Douay-Rheims Bible).[1] The two versions are, in fact, complementary to each other in rendering the original meaning.[2] In this verse, the wind is both substance and symbol; it makes God's presence palpable on one hand and, paradoxically, points to His absence (or, more accurately, His transcendental presence) on the other hand.

It is exactly the same interpretation that we encounter in the famous Akan proverb "As you speak to the wind, you speak to God" (Item 2656 in Christaller's collection),[3] the only difference being that the latter tends to emphasize the communicative aspect of man's relationship with deity, rather than deity's ultimate unpredictability and incomprehensibility which seems to dominate in the Gospel.

Thus, on the complete scale of gradation between materiality and spirituality, blood is naturally positioned in the middle and thus becomes a good candidate for the role of an intermediary between matter and spirit, as well as a general means of exchange between man and God. Indeed, it readily assumes the role of universal currency. Its natural *liquidity* makes this role all the more appropriate, especially if we remember that etymologically "currency" means the same thing—a physical/symbolic substance that *flows* from one party in return for a certain value (goods/service) to be provided by the other (from the Latin *currere* "to run, to flow").

Due to this status of spiritual currency, blood assumes a critical function in any *sacrifice* which originally means simply an act of exchange between man, who provides a substance otherwise unavailable to deity, and deity who provides assistance at things man cannot attain on his own. We should remember at this point that for the early (animistic) stages of human culture every economic activity can be viewed as sacrifice because on all occasions it necessarily involves interaction with deity (and usually cannot accomplish anything without divine involvement). It should be also noted that when the deity receives its remuneration for participation in the common cause (originally in the form of blood spilt during hunting) it is expected to

1. The Douay-Rheims Bible follows Jerome's version in the Latin Vulgate which preserves the original's use of cognates: *"Spiritus ubi vult spirat."*

2. An attempt to merge the double meaning of the Greek phrase is made in the Contemporary English Version which reads: "Only God's Spirit gives new life. The Spirit is like the wind that blows wherever it wants to."

3. Christaller. *A Collection of 3600 Twi Proverbs*, 1879.

consume it largely in the same manner as the hunter consumer his spoils. In such cases, blood is offered "by default," i.e., in the course of chasing and killing the animal, to the deity who on such occasions acts as the "beater"—by making the animal approach the hunter's ambush in return for the latter's prayers.

When people turn later to cattle herding and agriculture, this arrangement becomes more sophisticated. The role of deity in daily business activity is no longer so pronounced. Hunting an animal always requires good luck which is deity's responsibility to provide. Breeding an animal requires little else but industry and perhaps vigilance in warding off evil spirits. When the animal is slaughtered, deity's share can be easily overlooked or reduced in bad faith. To prevent it, special ceremonies have to be instituted. The transfer of blood from man to deity is no longer thought in terms of supply and consumption but in increasingly symbolic terms—as a means of renewing the original proximity (covenant) and continuing to enjoy divine support.

At even more advanced stages, this role of blood becomes purely symbolic: it still acts as a currency but entirely loses its material value. To draw a parallel from economics, we can say that this transformation is similar to that undergone by *money* which originally circulates in the form of gold coins or cowry shells (things that possess their own material value) but is later superseded by banknotes whose own value is negligible compared to the value of goods/services they can be exchanged for. Or, to put it in a figurative way, blood stops to be treated as "liquid gold" and becomes a spiritual "promissory note." This attitude is expressed, for example, in the later part of the already quoted verse from Leviticus (17:11): "for it *is* the blood *that* maketh an atonement for the soul." Here blood as a double-natured material/spiritual substance is subject to exchange in return for a purely spiritual favor on the part of deity—remission of man's sin (at this stage still understood as a legal trespass, rather than a moral wrong). The relationship becomes even more complicated once it receives a moral dimension which may compromise or even invalidate the exchange of material/spiritual values. The three examples that follow deal with typical adjustments/deviations to the originally straightforward process/rite of blood sacrifice.

1. Cain and Abel

This well-known story of sacrifice-turned-murder is told in the Book of Genesis (4:1–16). In the beginning, we have two brothers—Cain and Abel—performing their very different sacrifices. The younger one, who is a shepherd, slaughters the "firstlings of his flocks" and offers a typical blood sacrifice which is readily accepted by God. The elder one, who is "a tiller of the ground" offers a bloodless sacrifice—"the fruit of the ground"—thus substituting agricultural produce for animal blood. His offering is rejected and, after what we have told about the properties of various spiritual "currencies," is it easy to say why: fruit cannot compete with blood—it is solid and looks inanimate. You cannot "slaughter" a fruit in order to pass its spiritual essence on to deity. It is true that the juice of some fruits (grapes) bears striking resemblance to animal blood but, as we know from the Bible, viniculture has still to wait to be discovered until after the Flood (Gen 9:20).

Cain should have known better while choosing the right offering to God. He could either have asked his brother to supply an animal for the purpose and add his own fruit as a "side dish" to his sacrifice. Alternatively, perhaps as an even better option, he could have offered himself as a sacrificial victim. This would be in full accordance with Exodus 13:2 which says, "Sanctify unto me all the firstborn, whatsoever openeth the womb among the children of Israel, *both* of man and of beast: it *is* mine" and which means that as every eldest child Cain could be eligible for human sacrifice, even though this requirement does not seem to be strictly enforced at all times—cf. the famous exemption granted by God to Abraham with respect to his only begotten son Isaac (Gen 22:1–19).

Yet Cain is not satisfied with any of these "legitimate" options. Instead, he chooses Abel as a substitute, perhaps in the hope that the blood of a person so much favored by God would have a higher value in the "exchange" he is about to make. For a modern reader it may seem that Cain murders his brother out of envy—feeling offended by God's double standards. However, there is a hint in the Bible which allows us to suspect that this murder is ritual is character because, according to verse 8, it happens "when they were in the field"—probably, in that very field where the elder brother had been growing his crops and where he had recently offered his failed fruit sacrifice.

Yet the murder/sacrifice of Abel also proves a failure. Cain seems to have expected that his brother's blood would be accepted as a means of atonement without any regard to its provenance. He turns out to be mistaken. His offering is indeed accepted, although not by the sky god (Yahweh) but the earth goddess (most likely Yahweh's ancient consort—Asherah, although she is not mentioned here by name) who does not offer him anything in return but curses him instead:

> And now art thou cursed from the earth, which hath opened her mouth to receive thy brother's blood from thy hand (Gen 4:11)

Although the earth actually opens her mouth to swallow the sacrificial blood, it is the blood of the "wrong man." What was supposed to be an act of exchange from which Cain would expect extra favors for his business ends up in forfeiture. Not only will Cain receive no extra favors in return for his sacrifice (like more abundant rains or greater fertility of the soil he might have hoped to get)—he is also banned from further pursuing his trade, becoming "a fugitive and a vagabond . . . in the earth" (Gen 4:12). In other words, he must turn to cattle herding, i.e. adopt the trade of his murdered brother and the nomadic lifestyle associated with it in order to restore the lost balance—to offer the right sacrifice. To make sure he has a chance to redeem himself, he is granted full protection against being accidentally killed:

> And the Lord said unto him, Therefore whosoever slayeth Cain, vengeance shall be taken on him sevenfold. And the Lord set a mark upon Cain, lest any finding him should kill him (Gen 4:15).

Such is the high price for attempting to tamper with the established procedure of sacrifice.

2. Ywa Dɛnsu

From a very ancient text let us now turn to a very modern one. Modern not only in the sense that it comes from a recently published book but also that it describes a typically modern situation, when intentional and organized sacrifice tends to be neglected, first of all because today's people tend to overlook the necessity to contribute "blood currency" in exchange for maintenance of their welfare. Here is what the book says:[4]

> An Ɔbosom, Ywa Dɛnsu, revealed during a divination rite that whenever he feels he needs to drink blood, he takes two cars or buses—which look like small toys to him—from opposite directions and smash [sic] them together. Albeit spiritual acts, they invariably cause accidents. He would then squeeze and drink the blood of bad people, which he could easily identify. When asked what happens to the good people during accidents, his response was that he does not kill good people, as he examines those in the vehicles prior to his actions. But he admitted that some might be injured, although they always recover. And finally, when asked as to why blood, the emphatic response was "Blood is what I like."

"Ɔbosom" in the traditional religion of the Akan people is the term that commonly denotes a minor deity, subordinate to the Supreme Being

---

4. Ephirim-Donkor, *African Personality and Spirituality*, 74.

but nevertheless enjoying considerable independence in his actions. In the example above, feeling short of organized sacrifices offered to him by his votaries whose numbers have been steadily declining, the ɔbosom chooses to take the matter into his own hands and stage a traffic accident that would provide some blood for his consumption. Ywa Dɛnsu explicitly tells us what sort of consumption it is: it simply constitutes his meal. Even though (as we have seen in the previous section) it can also make him semiotically richer—by adding credit to his "blood account"—he is not aware of it or makes no mention to that effect. However, this is not so relevant for our study as the fact that in this case, as in the case of Cain and Abel, we have a moral dimension introduced into the story which involves both good and bad people.

The blood of righteous people has certainly a higher spiritual value or perhaps even a better nutritive value in the present example, just as the blood of the elder brother would be more valuable for the deity to consume in the example of Cain and Abel. However, unrestricted consumption of such blood would be possible only if it were offered *voluntarily*. Ywa Dɛnsu in our example, however, acts more like a debt collector than a party to a bargain—he makes people shed their blood against their will. He feels, therefore, bound to compensate for this largely immoral act by sparing the lives of good people. He grants them the same sort of immunity which the biblical God granted to Cain—by punishing them for improperly serving him (neglecting to sacrifice to him) and giving them a chance to redeem themselves at the same time.

Although many Christian readers may feel horrified at the outrageously barbaric behavior of Ywa Dɛnsu, they would hopefully treat it with more understanding when they discern a common semiotic pattern with the story of Cain and Abel, and perhaps even greater understanding after they see the example below.

3. Execution on Calvary

To a side observer, what happened on Calvary may look as a sacrifice *unilaterally* performed by God (i.e. without conscious human involvement) not for the purpose of nourishment (as consuming the blood of his own Son would mean committing an act of divine cannibalism) but for the sake of restoring the ancient proximity with man. Although the scales of these events differ significantly, we have here a very similar situation to the one described in the previous example: a deity disappointed by people's failure to honor an ancient covenant, takes the matter into his hands and stages an accident which, viewed superficially, looks like a mere punishment of a criminal but which, taken as an article of faith, has a far-reaching theological significance.

The circumstances of the Calvary event, as presented in the Gospel, look back to an even more ancient pattern than the story of Cain and Abel—the one of hunters' society. The sacrificial victim is identical with hunting game: it is stalked, chased, surrounded, and finally stabbed and hung on a tree as a trophy. His blood is collected into a vessel not to prevent it from being consumed by the earth, as it happened in the case of Abel, but to assure its delivery to the right consumer—first, to God himself (who consumes it only spiritually, as we remember) and then to man who, by tasting of that blood can partake of its divinity. Where the outsiders see only a traffic accident or execution of one accused of sedition and blasphemy, the initiated ones are able to behold an event of highly spiritual, even cosmic significance. Although the behavior of the Christian God looks much more humane and better planned in comparison with the amateurish feat of Ywa Dɛnsu, the similitude of the two cases is just as obvious: when humans display mismanagement or ineptness, the deity, through an act of "unperceived" sacrifice, is able to restore equity to the mutual benefit (propitiation and atonement) of the respective parties.

Indeed, Abraham's ominous words addressed to Isaac ("God will provide himself a lamb for a burnt offering," Gen 22:8) reveal their unexpectedly archaic meaning in this context—reinstituting deity in its original role of one who determines the success or failure of the hunting party, of one on whom *luck* depends. All this probably means that Christ can be regarded as the "Ram of God" (similar to the one found by Abraham as a substitute for Isaac—Gen 22:13), is no lesser degree that he is the Lamb of God. Although only the latter nomination seems to be used in Christian tradition, it is in discovering and analyzing the former one that we can more easily establish and assess parallels with African Traditional Religion.

Chapter VIII

Witchcraft

I HAVE (THANK GOD) no first-hand experience of witchcraft. Therefore, properly speaking, I cannot offer my own observations on the subject because, at the very best, it would only be observations of other people's observations which, still worse, are often not even observations but mere speculations. Witchcraft is notoriously elusive—to such an extent that many people (especially Westerners) deny it existence. On the other hand, considering how many people actually suffer from it, the question whether it is real or imaginary becomes irrelevant. Witchcraft is there, whatever one may think about its nature. This fact, as well as the hope that I may add a semiotic angle to the conversation, have enticed me to say a few words on the matter, even though my knowledge of it derives solely from books.

The main question which many authors writing about witchcraft seem to struggle to give an answer to is why the associated beliefs look so similar not only within Africa but also within regions which historically have had little contact with that continent (e.g., Melanesia).[1] In attempting a semiotic answer we should perhaps look for something just as universal in the history of mankind, something purely material to which witchcraft would provide a spiritual counterpart. Indeed, in most cases, a witch is believed to attack and consume the spiritual part of a human individual, his "spiritual organs," although eventually such an attack can result in causing harm

---

1. "But the real mystery to me is why African and Melanesian witchcraft beliefs, non-Biblical in their provenience, are, even in the era of Pentecostal incursion, so similar to each other," says Aletta Biersack in her afterword to the recently published collection *Pentecostalism and Witchcraft*, location 6325.

to his physical body as well. What, in that case, would be a purely bodily equivalent to witchcraft? The answer offers itself—it is cannibalism. Viewed semiotically, witchcraft and cannibalism seem to be originally parts of the same phenomenon—that of one human being consuming another. The two things initially stood with each other in the relation of a signified (cannibalism) to a signifier (witchcraft).

In modern times cannibalism has been mostly associated with Melanesia and its surrounding regions where ritual consumption of human flesh was attested as late as in 2012.[2] However, if we search for historical precedents, we shall quickly discover that cannibalism has been universal to humanity. We should also remember that at the earliest stages of human history there was no distinction between a ritual act and a profane act, as everything is sacred from the animistic point of view. We can see, for example, how common this practice was in Ancient Greece from a preserved fragment of Empedocles (c. 494—c. 434 BC):

> The father, lifting up his own son who has changed shape,
> Cuts his throat, with a prayer—fool that he is! The others are at a loss
> While they sacrifice the suppliant; but he, deaf to the shouts,
> Has cut the throat and prepared an evil meal in his house.
> In the same way, a son seizes his father and children their mother,
> And ripping out their life they devour the flesh of their dear ones.[3]

In the example above, it is irrelevant whether the acts described therein originate from the intention to offer a sacred meal to gods or simply to fill one's own stomach because there is no other food available. The sacrifice could indeed be offered in response to a shortage of animal or vegetable food (poor harvest or failed hunting) which would make the consumption of human flesh both a sacred and a profane act anyway. We can equally state that in this case the means of killing and consuming the victim are both material and spiritual. Thus, in the quoted fragment we observe both an act of cannibalism and an act of witchcraft in their primal unity.

At later development stages of certain human societies cannibalism may become a taboo. However, this taboo can be extended only to the material part of the practice, not its spiritual counterpart. As a result, when the signified is suppressed, the signifier becomes independent and turns into signified itself, acquiring its own signifier. Thus, the idea of witchcraft comes properly into existence when it stops being consciously associated with cannibalism,

---

2. The article on Wikipedia ("Human Cannibalism," https://en.wikipedia.org/wiki/Human_cannibalism) from which this information is taken references two contemporary sources to substantiate the claim: *New Zealand Herald* and *Smithsonian Magazine*.

3. Fragment B 137 = D 29 in the Diels-Kranz Edition.

while still preserving its original meaning of ritual/profane consumption/destruction of another individual. However, the means of accomplishing this act are now purely spiritual. Witches engage in spiritual cannibalism by leaving their own bodies in their sleep and entering their victims' habitation "in spirit" which can optionally be done by assuming the shape of a bird (an old soul symbol) or another nocturnal animal (with the same symbolic function).

In the quoted fragment from Empedocles, the acts of cannibalism are committed by the chief male in the family. Yet in many African societies (at least in West Africa) it is usually women who are accused of witchcraft. I find no contradiction here. When physical cannibalism stops being socially acceptable, its mental reflection becomes marginalized and passes on to more "inferior" members of society. Besides, in modern West Africa at least, it is normally the woman who is in charge of preparing meals, which should contribute to her being regarded as someone more exposed to the temptation to use human flesh for feeding her family in the time of famine and, by extension, indulging herself in the practice of witchcraft at other times. Thus, we can say that both cannibalism and witchcraft can be regarded as unintentional relapses into animality which can be later sanctioned as para-religious acts, although, as we remember, the duty of any religion is to prevent that sort of relapse.

Witchcraft is often considered to be hereditary, i.e. passing from mother to daughter (less frequently from father or mother to son) without need of any training to acquire that ability on achieving adulthood. In this respect it is opposed to sorcery which is usually acquired by training, rather than inherited. Also, sorcery seems to be more intentional in its application, while witchcraft often seems to exist on the subconscious level. How much all this can allow us to assert that both cannibalism and witchcraft are "hard-wired" in human genome is difficult to say as no research, to my knowledge, has ever been conducted in that field.

Whether witchcraft is real or imaginary in a given society is not the semiotician's concern. It can remain "real" as long as it keeps being "committed" in the witch's or victim's mind. What should be, however, of greater interest to us is that in different societies witchcraft seems to assume a more universal status than in others. In West Africa, as we have noted, it is mostly attributed to elderly women, i.e. those members of society who are semiotically perceived to be most prone to relapsing into animality. On the other hand, if we are to trust the scholarly authority of E. E. Evans-Pritchard (1902–73), among some peoples of East Africa (Azande in this case)[4] witch-

---

4. I refer to his famous 1937 book *Witchcraft, Oracles and Magic Among the Azande* of which I have used the abridged edition of 1976, the original being hard to come by.

craft is believed to be a universally spread phenomenon that plagues their society irrespective of gender.

What we observe in this case is the common tendency towards generalization of the sign used to express the idea of evil. Evil tends to be personified in many religions. It often derives from some deity originally responsible for something that caused pain or any other inconvenience. This spirit (deity) gradually monopolizes all uncomfortable associations until it finally becomes a universal image and a sole person responsible to all manifestations of evil. This is, for example, what happened to Beelzebub: originally the Lord of the Flies (probably the most common pest in the Near East) it became a universal symbol of dark powers and in this shape was borrowed by Judaism as a chief antagonist of YHWH. The Zande situation is, however, different. Their Supreme Being playing only an insignificant role in their religion, their symbols of good and evil became less personified in appearance. Thus, the universal symbol of evil devolves to witchcraft which comes to impersonate a nondescript substance that enables anyone envious of his neighbor's possessions or success in life to cause harm to the latter, often even without any conscious intent.

Yet this universalization is also known to Judaism and perhaps reflects an earlier stage in the development of that religion when it is emerges in the last (tenth) commandment of the Decalogue, following the orders not to commit adultery, not to steal and not to bear false witness:

> Thou shalt not covet thy neighbour's house, thou shalt not covet thy neighbour's wife, nor his manservant, nor his maidservant, nor his ox, nor his ass, nor any thing that is thy neighbour's (Exod 20:17).

The prohibition to "covet" is enforced so strictly here not because it is simply immoral to dream about taking over from one's neighbor but because entertaining these sinful desires can result in actual harm being caused to that neighbor. Evil wishes are interpreted as potentially constituting unintentional and perhaps even unconscious "witchcraft." Much in the same way as the ninth commandment is intended to address the abuse of words (signs) with which we speak, the last one tackles the abuse of signs with which we think. While the former is based on the well-known *dictum–factum* rule, the latter, we can say, expands the same rule to things said in one's mind only and can thus be conventionally styled "*cogitatum–factum.*" Thus, what constitutes such abuse in the case of Judaism corresponds to the abuse of individual spiritual powers that give rise to witchcraft among the Zande.

It remains to be added that the same concept of mental harm (although with more accent on self-harm in this case) can be discerned in Jesus' Sermon on the Mount, in that part of it which concerns adultery:

> Ye have heard that it was said by them of old time, Thou shalt not commit adultery: But I say unto you, That whosoever looketh on a woman to lust after her hath committed adultery with her already in his heart (Matt 5:27–28).

Following the same logic, we can add with the same degree of certainty that whoever thinks of stealing one's neighbor's ox or ass, or anything else that he may covet, has already committed theft of that article in his mind too.

Although Jesus is obviously preoccupied with the moral aspect of "thought crime" in this example, he proceeds on the same premise as Moses in the Decalogue or, indeed, as a common Zande person in his fear of witchcraft: equaling evil intention with its materialization. It also means that the Sermon of the Mount, although quite justifiably regarded as a piece of revolutionary thinking, is in many respects based on highly conservative traditional approaches. We shall come back to this issue again in the chapter on the semiotic message of Jesus.

As noted above, not all African religions reach the same level of generalization—when any egoistic (animal) impulse, if not nipped in the bud, can result in irreparable damage to the object of antisocial desires and eventually to the evil thinker himself. However, we can say that the same pattern underlies both traditionalist and monotheistic approach to the problem. An unsuppressed subconscious impulse towards cannibalism and a highly conscious hope of getting away undetected and unpunished for entertaining sinful thoughts and dreams can trigger the same mechanism of action/retribution based on the primal identity of signifier and signified. This, in my opinion, is exactly what accounts for the striking similarity in the witchcraft ideas that are common for many religions of various geographically remote regions.

Viewed from that perspective, the sudden resurgence of witch-hunting in the post-Renaissance Europe should no longer surprise us that much. The seventeenth century in that region was the age when the notion of private property as opposed to collective ownership comes to the foreground in all its naked sharpness. The emergent capitalism and the speedy enrichment of certain groups of people, seemingly at the expense of others, brought about an enormous tangle of envious wishes whose supernatural aspect was still not quite forgotten. The inaccessibility of one's neighbor's assets resulted in a cannibalistic wish to consume them mentally, physically or both ways. Another person's physical body in that case simply acts as a semiotic substitute for his possessions. Imported into Africa to its full extent in the twentieth century, capitalism has significantly contributed to the exponential growth of witchcraft thinking on the continent.

However, as I noted at the start of this chapter, having no personal exposure to this phenomenon, I can present my discussion on witchcraft as nothing but a passing digression. Let us now go back to more essential considerations that would allow us to proceed with our comparative study of related but not quite identical semiotic systems. One of the most essential ones in this context would be the controversial issue of polytheism vs monotheism.

Chapter IX

Polytheism and Monotheism: Absorption vs Diffusion

THE FAMOUS AND NOW widely accepted definition of African religion as "diffused monotheism" given by E. Bọlaji Idowu (1913–1993) in *Olódùmarè*[1] is essentially correct but can be misleading because it tells only half of the story; in fact, the second half of it only. It takes the idea of a single God as a starting point, as something that has always been in place. In reality, however, this idea is a product of a long evolution which begins at the animistic stage and carries on well into the modern times. The evolution consists in the process of one deity gradually ousting all others and finally setting in as an autocratic Supreme Being. This process can be conveniently termed "absorption." However, no sooner than the absorption is complete, it is almost immediately followed by its opposite—the process of a monotheistic deity acquiring a "retinue," i.e. exchanging his transcendency for immanence. This is exactly what constitutes the *diffusion* as defined and described by Idowu. We are going to discuss both processes in detail below due to their high importance in understanding the relationship between polytheism and monotheism.

---

1. Idowu, *Olódùmarè*, 204.

1. Absorption

As we noted in the "Origin" chapters, initially, at the stage conventionally known as "animism" we have a perfect correspondence between the thing (object, person, phenomenon) and its name (symbol, spirit, soul). As soon as a new object comes into man's field of vision, it must be named; but receiving a name also means being automatically assigned a certain deity (spirit) in charge of that thing. Problems start when human eyesight becomes so much refined and detailed that its spiritual counterpart begins to struggle in catching up. The numberless spirits and deities that spring up into existence as a result have to be arranged relative to each other, with priorities and hierarchies established in order to prevent lapsing into complete chaos.

This task is not easy. One and the same thing can acquire multiple names (synonymy). Different things may be called by the same name (homonymy). Parts of things may receive separate names but then: 1) one of the parts can extrapolate its name to the whole thing, ousting its previous name (synecdoche); or 2) parts of a previous whole can begin to be treated as independent items (analysis); or 3) previously discrete items can be united under the umbrella of a more general notion (synthesis). Still another common option: the name (symbol, soul, daemon) can gain greater independence from the thing it designates and start living a life of its own, rambling at large (often at night-time), acquiring its own symbols or taking possession of objects it initially had no claims over.

There seems to be no end to the possible ways in which matter and spirit, body and soul, thing and symbol can lose sight of each other, move apart or form "dangerous liaisons" with other objects. One of the earliest known examples of this situation is vividly presented in the story of the Tower of Babel (Gen 11:1–9). From semiotic perspective, it is simply a story how an attempt to preserve or restore the original unity between humanity and divinity (building a structure to reconnect man with God) using manmade means (artefacts) can result in an even greater confusion. It is true that in this example the situation is exacerbated by the cosmopolitan nature of the Babylonian civilization. However, it applies just as well to a monolingual culture whose technological development is advanced enough to create problems in designating its own achievements. The primeval unity of meaning and expression disintegrates due to the increasing complexity of the system fraught with its own internal conflicts and perhaps even further destabilized by possible strife among various community members/generations who may easily offer conflicting designations of the same thing.

Once the problem is realized, the construction project is abandoned. Man sees now that it is the spiritual, not the material world that requires streamlining and rearrangement. The remedy is finally found in making more general ideas dominate over more particular ones. Thus the initial confusion that reigns in people's minds at the sight of endless spirits that surround them gives way to a better organized hierarchy presided by a supreme ruler who, for a while, is occupied with nothing else but subjugating and later eliminating his rivals. The original horror at the enormous task facing the primitive theologian—to sort out the numerous numinous beings—is replaced by the awe experienced in contemplating a generalization that is able to put an end to the previous anarchy of independent spiritual subjects. Yet this generalization comes at a price, because it raises the question of universality vs specialization. In the passage from Augustine of Hippo (354–430) quoted below this underlying sense of uneasiness at making the final step into monotheism is obvious in spite the attempt to jam it by passionately indignant idiom:

> But how is it possible to recount in one part of this book all the names of gods or goddesses, which they could scarcely comprise in great volumes, distributing among these divinities their peculiar offices about single things? They have not even thought that the charge of their lands should be committed to any one god: but they have entrusted their farms to Rusina; the ridges of the mountains to Jugatinus; over the downs they have set the goddess Collatina; over the valleys, Vallonia. Nor could they even find one Segetia so competent, that they could commend to her care all their corn crops at once; but so long as their seed-corn was still under the ground, they would have the goddess Seia set over it; then, whenever it was above ground and formed straw, they set over it the goddess Segetia; and when the grain was collected and stored, they set over it the goddess Tutilina, that it might be kept safe. Who would not have thought that goddess Segetia sufficient to take care of the standing corn until it had passed from the first green blades to the dry ears? Yet she was not enough for men, who loved a multitude of gods, that the miserable soul, despising the chaste embrace of the one true God, should be prostituted to a crowd of demons.[2]

We can say, however, that Augustine's indignation is largely misplaced due to the fact that he introduces a moral dimension where there was none originally. Indeed, from the purely semiotic perspective, what Augustine describes here seems to be the only feasible way for a primitive agriculturalist to assure success of his enterprise. The more detailed the latter's knowledge

2. Augustine, *The City of God*, book VI, chapter 8.

of the vegetation cycle, the better chance for him to keep it under control. Yet "detailed knowledge" in the primal sense of the phrase means nothing else but close interaction with the spiritual entity (demon) responsible for each respective part of that cycle. The interaction starts with assigning proper names to those actors and later seeking their favors at each respective stage. The impressive list of deities in charge of the growth of a single ear of corn testifies to nothing else but thorough *analytical* work conducted by the primitive agriculturalist in his proto-scientific study of the crop. "Proto-scientific" because, unlike modern science, here every material component successfully identified by the cultivator invariably comes with its spiritual counterpart (name of the demon in charge). It is only after this analysis is complete (to the fullest possible extent allowed by the current state of the art) that *synthesis* becomes possible and the whole cycle/process can now be transferred into the competence of a single actor (monotheistic deity) who is now believed to be capable of combining the totality of skills previously assumed to reside in exclusive competence of specialized deities.

In general, such a proto-scientific method is consistently employed in all essential human activities that involve interaction with nature, including, obviously, hunting and livestock-breeding. Below is an example of the established procedure to be employed by Australian aborigines while engaging in one of those activities, as recorded by Spencer and Gillen in the late ninetieth century:

> When a clever man is out hunting and comes across the tracks of, say, a kangaroo, he follows them along and talks to the footprints all the time for the purpose of injecting magic into the animal which made them. He mentions in succession *all the parts of the foot, and then names the different parts of the leg right up to the animal's back*. As soon as he reaches the backbone, the creature becomes quite stupid and is an easy prey.[3]

In the above example, mentioning the animal's body parts plays the same role as the successive invocation of plant formations during the vegetation cycle. The goal in both cases is to obtain control over the target object by means of correct naming (addressing) its constituent material/spiritual entities.

We witness the very outset of this procedure in Genesis 2:18–20 which describes it in a very clear and succinct fashion:

---

3. Quoted from Lucien Lévy-Bruhl, *How Natives Think*, location 3142. Emphasis added.

> And the Lord God said, It is not good that the man should be alone; I will make him an help meet for him. And out of the ground the Lord God formed every beast of the field, and every fowl of the air; and brought them unto Adam to see what he would call them: and whatsoever Adam called every living creature, that was the name thereof. And Adam gave names to all cattle, and to the fowl of the air, and to every beast of the field ...

Note in the passage above that it is not God but Adam who undertakes the task to produce names for each animal he encounters. The reason is obvious: it is only in the process of interacting with the creatures (i.e. enlisting their *help*) that man is able to come up with the relevant names for them. It is only after *analyzing* his surroundings and establishing a link of each *animal* with its *anima* by working out its name that Adam can proceed to *synthesis* which results in developing his relationship with nature as a whole and gradually assimilate it to culture.

Both the Australian and biblical examples clearly show that analysis necessarily precedes synthesis in human cognition. The examples also prove that it is erroneous to assume that a general idea of spirituality originally exists as some nondescript impression on human mind, of which the practitioner of primal religion can say nothing definite. This postulated shapeless reality is often referred to as *mana*. This term, originally of Melanesian stock, has been extrapolated by some anthropologists to serve as a universal expression of man's primal encounter with "the Other." Yet, this very "otherness" is in fact the product of centuries-long interaction analysis of man's perceptions and interactions—a very sophisticated abstract notion which expresses the unity of things which man's ultimate synthesis has been able to assimilate and, on the other hand, those which it has failed to process. It includes both things in man's bright field of vision and those beyond it ("the Other").

Going back to the above-quoted passage from Augustine, we can say that the same analytical pattern can be used in defense of polytheism, even if we choose to accept the moral grounds on which the bishop of Hippo prefers to launch his attack. One may well say in retaliation that putting "one true God" in charge of such petty chores as grain sprouting or straw formation looks no less like "prostituting" him than leaving them to the discretion of "demons," each of which is a perfect expert on his own narrow field. Would not the latter cope better with the tasks exclusively assigned to each of them, without the need for the Supreme Being to bother? Thus, monotheism, as soon as it completes the process of absorption becomes ready for diffusion, i.e. for the Supreme Being to delegate his various routine tasks to his subordinates. Yet, as we shall see later, the process of diffusion is built on a different basis and produces different results than the original animism.

One of the reasons for this difference is the fact that the Supreme Being engaged in the process of absorption acquires not only universal wisdom but also universal goodness, thus making radically different the perception of good and evil between the animistic and theistic views. Originally, no distinction between good and evil is made at all and only power is appreciated. When the world around us starts to receive a moral dimension, the latter also tends to be monopolized by the Supreme Being. Let Augustine speak again to illustrate that point:

> A pretty decree of the senate it was, truly, by which the temple of Concord was built on the spot where that disastrous rising had taken place, and where so many citizens of every rank had fallen. [. . .] For if they had any regard to consistency, why did they not rather erect on that site a temple of Discord? Or is there a reason for Concord being a goddess while Discord is none? Does the distinction of Labeo hold here, who would have made the one a good, the other an evil deity?—a distinction which seems to have been suggested to him by the mere fact of his observing at Rome a temple to Fever as well as one to Health. But, on the same ground, Discord as well as Concord ought to be deified. [. . .] Those wise and learned men are enraged at our laughing at these follies; and yet, being worshippers of good and bad divinities alike, they cannot escape this dilemma about Concord and Discord: either they have neglected the worship of these goddesses, and preferred Fever and War, to whom there are shrines erected of great antiquity, or they have worshipped them, and after all Concord has abandoned them, and Discord has tempestuously hurled them into civil wars.⁴

The original arrangement so much ridiculed by Augustine was to worship the good gods and propitiate the evil ones. From that point of view there is nothing wrong in erecting a temple to Discordia or, if we want an African example, nothing wrong about worshiping Sopona, the god of smallpox who must certainly be propitiated in order to avoid the spread of that dangerous disease. However, this can be done with assurance only as long as religion enjoys the status of being *beyond good and evil*. When the difference between the two things finally asserts itself, only good powers become worth worshipping. These powers are generalized and absorbed by

---

4. Augustine, *The City of God*, book III, chapter 25.

the universal idea of goodness—the monotheistic God, while evil is either declared "non-substantial" (*privatio boni*) or allocated to the sphere of evil powers, ultimately leading to the rise of a dualistic system. The question of the origin of evil in such cases usually remains without a final answer. Thus both absolute wisdom and absolute goodness prove to be unstable formations and initiate the process of diffusion, once their realization is achieved. This process will be our concern in the next section.

2. Diffusion

As we noted in the previous section, the process of diffusion starts almost immediately after (or perhaps even before) the Supreme Being has completed his transformation from a deity competing with others for primacy to the sole autocrat of the universe. In many religions this role is assumed and fulfilled by the *sky god*, hence the special character of the diffusion it later undergoes. Let us see now how this may actually happen.

The sky god indeed looks like a perfect candidate for the role of the Supreme Being. The sky covers the largest part of visible space, it never moves and is placed above the earth, which naturally suggests the idea of subordination. Things that cease to exist in the terrestrial world tend to be believed to vanish into thin air, i.e. received (absorbed) by the sky. The sky is usually designated by a circle—symbol just as universal, understandable, and acceptable as its signified.

The diffusion of the sky god can proceed along different lines. One possible scenario is when it is suggested by observations of the sky itself and the changes it undergoes day and night, as well as over the year. The monthly changes of the moon on the night sky, for instance, create an especially favorable background for the process. Every new moon is observable only for a limited number of days after which it disappears and is later replaced by another one which is bound to disappear just as its predecessor. Yet, once the year completes its full circle, everything seems to repeat itself in the same order as in the previous year. Hence the conclusion that the moons observable in the new year are not new but the same ones that appeared in turn on the sky exactly a year ago. This reduces their number to nine (the original number of months in the calendar) or (more commonly) twelve.

These rotating moons become perfect candidates for forming the retinue of the sky god. They are his monthly incarnations serving in turns but at the same time always present and ready to take over the watch. Their "reflexes" in various mythologies and religions are ubiquitous. Among the Greeks, we have the example of Apollo (originally a sky god who was later displaced by other deities and reassigned to a different field of occupation) accompanied by *nine* Muses whose number testifies to origin from the old calendar and whose distribution of duties in art patronage is a very late invention. This archaic pantheon of the diffused sky god is later replaced by the more up-to-date twelve-member pantheon of the Olympians. In Judaism this set finds its correspondence in the twelve archangels, while in Christianity we have their earthly reflex in the twelve Apostles.

The pattern persists even when it no longer represents the sky god as such but his terrestrial impression reproduced in various historical (or quasi-historical) tales and political institutions. Thus, we have the twelve tribes of Israel—descendants of the twelve original retainers of the sky god, later turned into cultural heroes; twelve lictors accompanying the Roman consul and twelve paladins that compose the retinue of both Charlemagne and King Arthur.

At first, the members of the divine retinue are completely indistinguishable from each other—they have no more individuality then the moons that appear in turn on the night sky within their apportioned terms of service. Over time, however, at least some of them try to rise over the indistinct "mass" and assert their uniqueness. Some of the paladins become more distinguished for their bravery, some, on the other hand, for their meanness (Ganelon in the Charlemagne cycle, Judas in Christianity). This is probably because some of them were originally in charge of those months which fell on more or less favorable agricultural seasons.

The Apostle Peter, for example, whose feast day is traditionally celebrated in June, possibly rose to prominence for that reason. Other Jesus' disciples, as we know, are notorious for their attempts to claim privileged seats in the future Kingdom of God. It may be not quite by chance that it was no one else but the sons of Zebedee, James and John, whose feast days fall on opposite times of the year—July and December respectively—who dared ask their master "Let one of us sit at your right and the other at your left in your glory" (Mark 10:37). It is true that Jesus as well as the other disciples immediately rebuke them for their ambitions but the very fact that such an idea could come to their mind is nevertheless remarkable. As for Judas Iscariot, his attempts to stand out among the "faceless" mass of other disciples are too well-known to be described in detail.

The tendency towards greater individuality, or, in other words, towards more "densely" diffused monotheism becomes more pronounced with the appearance of a shorter, weekly, time cycle—certainly a much later phenomenon that the annual one. The origin of the seven-day week is too difficult a question to be discussed here. What we should rather like to note on this occasion is that each day of the week seems—quite early in history—to be given to an individual deity to patronize. Thus, the Latin names for those days (from which the English names also ultimately derive) correspond to the seven gods specially selected for the purpose. Those deities, as it is well-know, also double as celestial bodies, which implies that originally such a selection may not have been random. Starting from Sunday, they are, respectively, the Sun, the Moon, Mars, Mercury, Jupiter, Venus, and Saturn. They are all bright individualities and one of them—Jupiter—obviously claims a paramount status, as he also doubles as the sky god.

If we were now to take an African example for comparison, we would almost certainly land on the proper names linked with the weekly cycle in the Akan religion. Here we have not one but two sets of names in correspondence with each day—the male and female ones. The first is Kwasi, Kwadwo, Kwabena, Kwaku, Yaw, Kofi, and Kwame; the second, respectively, Akosua, Adwoa, Abenaa, Akua, Yaa, Afua, and Ama. Their origin is disputable and their individual differences cannot be easily traced. However, they are quite likely to be originally the names of certain deities. It is hard to tell which stage of evolution we observe in this case: 1) It may be that the process of diffusion is only at its embryonic phase and what we have here is just a "faceless" list with no individuality attached to its members as yet—similar to the initial list of the apostles where the evangelist's only concern seems to be to assure the "compulsory" number twelve with no accent on individuality. (What do we know, for example, about the personalities of such people as Philip or Jude, except that they had different names, apart from later apocryphal stories told about them?) 2) It may be on the contrary that the divinity of those persons has been absorbed by the advancing monotheistic deity, changing the "day gods" into mere signs without much reference to their original background. I find both scenarios equally possible because I think that the forces of both absorption and diffusion are simultaneously operating in any given religion.

Can we find anything to match these weekly designations in Christianity? I think that in order to do so we should turn our attention to a very detailed description of a certain week presented by all four Gospels—the Holy Week—and see whether we can spot any differences between the stories traditionally associated with its specific days. It is true that none of the Gospels gives a daily breakdown of the events they place within that brief but eventful timeframe. We do not know for sure, for example, on which day Jesus performed his famous Cleansing of the Temple or was anointed by Mary of Bethany. But perhaps the very nature of those events can give us some clues about the ancient deities that lurk on their background, deities about to be absorbed by the God of the new covenant.

It is certain that Jesus himself would hardly care for this takeover because he was a Jew. The Jewish calendar has no names, much less personalities, associated with the days of the week. The days are simply called "first," "second," etc. with the exception of Saturday which is referred to as "the day of rest." However, for the authors of the Gospels, things might have looked different. They were writing their books with Gentile readers in mind, therefore they used Greek, not Aramaic, for the purpose. It is true that they could do so to be better understood by the Jewish diaspora scattered over the Roman Empire. Yet the Jews living in diaspora could be more susceptible to external influences and therefore better prepared to take in some Gentile ideas, if only to be more firmly convinced in their inferiority to their own values. In other words, it is not unthinkable that the Gospel authors could view at least some of Jesus' actions during the Holy Week as steps taken towards the absorption of divine signification of its separate days. The two examples given below can show, I believe, that this statement is not completely unfounded.

3. Holy Tuesday

It is traditionally assumed that on that day Jesus foretold his own death (John 12:20–36, repeated in John 13:21–38). We also remember that in the mind of the evangelist there is a steady association between the destruction of (or at least damage to) Jesus' physical body and the structure of the Jerusalem Temple (John 2:21). We can say, therefore, that there is a strong link between Jesus' prophecy of his own death and his pronouncement on the fate of the Temple, Jewish nation, and perhaps human race in general given in Matthew 24, Mark 13 and Luke 21:

> Now the brother shall betray the brother to death, and the father the son; and children shall rise up against their parents, and shall cause them to be put to death (Mk 13:12).

Is it pure coincidence that the scenes of violence described in Jesus' prophecy should be presented on the day dedicated to Mars, the god of war? Can it mean that the evangelist wants Jesus to take over from that god, so that from then on all wars will be waged between the righteous and the unrighteous "for my name's sake" (Mk 13:13)? If so, Tuesday would be a very appropriate day to make such statements. We can take it still further and suggest that the only act of violence committed by Jesus in the Gospel—the Cleansing of the Temple—was likelier to happen on Tuesday, rather than on Monday.

4. Spy Wednesday

While we spoke in a very cautious manner about the possible events of Holy Tuesday, we can speak with greater confidence about Spy Wednesday whose very name reflects the tradition to associate this day with Judas' betrayal of Jesus. Wednesday, as we remember, is dedicated to Mercury who is both a divine messenger and a trickster god. This is quite normal, for, as we also remember, messengers and tricksters are often combined in one person (cf. the ambiguous role of the Serpent who also betrays God's trust by leaking some "classified" information to man in Genesis 3:4–5). It is remarkable that Judas acts exactly the same part of trickster-messenger by revealing Jesus' whereabouts to the authorities, thus prompting the latter's arrest and execution. Yet this "playing Mercury" causes his own speedy downfall because it is Jesus, not Judas, who is actually in control now, even though no one around seems to notice it:

> Jesus answered, He it is, to whom I shall give a sop, when I have dipped it. And when he had dipped the sop, he gave it to Judas Iscariot, the son of Simon. And after the sop Satan entered into him. Then said Jesus unto him, That thou doest, do quickly. Now no man at the table knew for what intent he spake this unto him. For some of them thought, because Judas had the bag, that Jesus had said unto him, Buy those things that we have need of against the feast; or, that he should give something to the poor. He then having received the sop went immediately out: and it was night (John 13:26–30).

Going through the entire Holy Week to map out its probable correspondences with the pagan weekly cycle would be a fascinating exercise which would, however, require a separate study. I hope the above examples are enough to form an idea about the forces of absorption/diffusion at play on the pages of the New Testament.

We can only add that at still more advanced stages of development, the Holy Week is complemented and in some respects even superseded by the liturgical year—when each day, without exception and often without any connection to the Gospel events, is assigned a name and a patron saint in charge of it. Thus the Christian God becomes perfectly and evenly diffused over the annual cycle. Every day is sanctified by receiving its own hierophanic signifier, even though, as we have seen above, some of these signifiers claim to have a greater share in the divine diffusion than others.

Those Protestant denominations which admit no veneration of saints tend to oppose this diffusion in which they—quite rightly—perceive the danger of sliding into polytheism. What they achieve, however, by suppressing this "common" process is a relapse to animism, when the deity which has previously absorbed the divine essence of his rivals, being unable to diffuse it, starts to "desorb" it back into the environment. Hence the numerous "nature cults" which have been persistently originating at least since the eighteenth century almost exclusively from thinkers with a Protestant background (Rousseau, etc.). Such cults currently predominate the consciousness of contemporary Western society where an offense against Nature entails by far greater opprobrium than an offence against God who has largely faded into insignificance:

> Once blasphemy against God was the greatest blasphemy; but God died, and therewith also those blasphemers. To blaspheme the earth is now the dreadfulest sin, and to rate the heart of the unknowable higher than the meaning of the earth! (Nietzsche, *Thus Spake Zarathustra*, translated by Thomas Common, Part One, Zarathustra's Discourses, 3)

This is because modern Western society has been largely shaped by the predominantly protestant ideologies of the industrial powers that determined its cultural priorities in the last couple of centuries.

With all of the above taken into account, we can now venture the following preliminary conclusion: The initial animistic entities which constitute precise spiritual correspondences to material objects of the surrounding reality gradually give way to an increasingly generalized idea/entity which tends to deprive the former, first of their spiritual essence reducing them to mere names and finally eliminating them completely. From this point of view, animism is the object (substratum) of that absorption and can be defined as "primary polytheism," "unabsorbed polytheism," or "potential monotheism."

Once the absorption is complete, the universal entity (usually the sky god) tends to diffuse itself into natural phenomena from which it previously withdrew itself (as the sky god delegating his authority), thus giving rise to various attendants, legates, and servants that form the Supreme Being's retinue with various degrees of homogeneity among its members. The status achieved thereby can be styled "secondary polytheism" or "diffused monotheism."

Both "absorbed animism" and "diffused monotheism" are usually present in any given religion and determine the dynamic equilibrium which results from the interaction of the above two forces at a given point of time.

Obviously, their specific relation would be unique for each religion, where absorption can currently predominate over diffusion or vice versa. However, there is no religion, in our opinion, where both these forces/processes would not be active. To oppose African Traditional Religion to Christianity as polytheism to monotheism is not just old-fashioned or politically incorrect; it is simply wrong.

Chapter X

The Twilight of the Gods

ALTHOUGH THE PHRASE USED in the title of this chapter is probably based on misinterpretation of the Icelandic word "Ragnarök" which most likely means "doom of the gods" rather than their "twilight," one has to admit that the error has been an extremely lucky one as the phrase comes in handy to introduce our next subject—the *loss of signification* undergone by divine beings in all religions without exception. I say that the mistake is "fortunate" because the word used to render "Ragnarök" into English (originally into German by Richard Wagner as "*Götterdämmerung*") has an important semiotic aspect. "Twilight" refers to such a state of luminosity when it becomes impossible for the human eye to distinguish colors and when shapes start to melt into the background, i.e. when objects begin to lose their perceived identity.

All deities are doomed to face their "twilight" sooner or later. This is not because human beings grow more skeptical and lose their faith in the supernatural—as we shall see from the chapter where we discuss atheism, beliefs in the supernatural may get only stronger with the advancement of civilization. This is rather because any symbol, any image, any visual impression tends to wear out over time. Gods disappear because, being always present, they stop being noticed. This process is intensified by the fact that the means of expression originally employed by man to designate divine nature keep reminding him of their inadequacy.

The sky god is especially vulnerable to this process as he resides in an element (the sky) which is quite poor and often controversial in its means of signification. Although it looks more uniform than the earth below, its constantly driving clouds in the daytime and rotating celestial bodies at night suggest that it is too changeable to be a generalized expression of stability and reliability. The sky's behavior often does not make sense—its weather and climate vagaries seem too whimsical, unmotivated and even cruel. The sky's face does not look intelligent enough—it is often too plain, too empty of expression to represent divine intelligence. Compared with the sky, the earth looks steadier with its mountains, deserts, rivers, oceans that never move, and its forests and fields that change only seasonally. Yet the earth makes an even poorer God's abode because it completely deprives him of transcendency.

Quite often, to look more intelligent, a god may become anthropomorphic. This is only logical. Man, after all, seems to be the most intelligent visible creature, however willing he may be initially to conceal his intelligence and make other animals (totems) parade the scene in his stead. Nevertheless, he still presents the best image to stand for a superior and intelligent power. This is why anthropomorphism eventually overcomes zoomorphism wherever man chooses to come out with what he truly thinks of himself. However, anthropomorphism is just as ill-suited to stand the "transcendency test" as anything else that suggests an earthly object. The more the idea of transcendency comes to the foreground in a given religion, the less anthropomorphism is perceived as appropriate. On the other hand, the more inaccessible and unapproachable the Supreme Being is, the easier it is to make him solely responsible for everything, even if it runs contrary to reason. The Supreme Being must remain transcendent to ensure the conversion of apparent arbitrariness into divine providence. This requirement does not encourage the deity to retain his anthropomorphic shape for too long.

Finally, the stage is reached where neither the sky, nor the human body can hold the whole of the Supreme Being. One starts to suspect that something is hidden behind the traditional representations current in religion, something that can be expressed neither in words nor in images. The only means of signification left at man's disposal cannot be pictographic anymore—and this includes the sky, the earth, and man himself. They can now only be ideographic, i.e. they should bear absolutely no resemblance to any real object. This is what happens to the signification of YHWH in Judaism. But even that solution can be regarded only as a temporary one. In the end, the Supreme Being is bound to part with all signification. No sign is adequate the express the notion of an all-powerful and omnipresent God who is transcendent and immanent at the same time, who is responsible for the creation of the world and maintaining its integrity on a daily and even hourly basis. The absolute nature of such an entity comes into conflict with the conventional nature of all signs at human disposal. This conflict is deeply felt by many religions most of which tend to come up with some sort of compromise between the desire to find an appropriate symbol for God and the realization of the futility (and even sinfulness) of that attempt.

If we look at the situation in non-Abrahamic religions, we shall easily observe their sky gods at various stages of disappearance (=loss of signification). We can take as our first example the Proto-Indo-European sky deity whose reconstructed name is *Dyeus. Among his numerous reflexes in various linguistic branches that derive from this common source, only the Greek Zeus and Roman Jupiter preserve the paramount status of that deity to the full extent. Yet, even in Greek mythology, Zeus is a next-generation god who has displaced his heavenly father Cronus, most likely because he has come into possession of a weapon (the lightning) which has made him semiotically much more visible than his predecessor (who is probably himself of non-Indo-European origin). Zeus was lucky in that respect, we may say, because the ability to wield the lightning was not among the original attributes of this proto-deity.

The Vedic religion of India retains only weak traces of this originally chief god in the name of Dyáuṣ Pitṛ́ whose personality, whatever it was in the beginning, appears almost completely dissolved. However, the most interesting case is probably provided by the Scandinavian deity Tyr (Proto-Germanic *Tiwaz) whose name also derives from the original Indo-European figure. Apart from being a relatively unimportant god without any steady occupation, who never managed to master the use of the lightning (this ability devolved to Thor), he is often depicted with one hand missing. Whatever the alleged noble motive for losing his hand (he is believed to have sacrificed it in order to overcome the wolf Fenrir—the embodiment of the universal evil) this is an obvious sign of the process of semiotic disappearance being rather advanced. Tyr is due to die at Ragnarök (together with all the other principal deities) in order to give way to the next generation of gods and thus complete the cycle of renewal.

If we now turn to Africa, we shall see a very similar picture. Take Olódùmarè, the "God in Yoruba belief," according to Idowu. That deity retains the status of chief creator as well as master of all the other deities and spirits. Yet, apart from his name, the means of signification at his disposal are extremely scarce. Let us see how Idowu describes the fast disappearing ritual which he could probably still witness himself or at least know from first-hand sources:

> Because Olódùmarè cannot be confined into space, the ritualistic worship offered to Him takes place in the open. The worshiper makes a circle of *ashes or white chalk*; within the circle, which is a symbol of eternity, he pours a libation of *cold* water, and in the centre he places his kola-nut on *cotton wool*. He then takes the kola-nut, splits it and holding the valves firmly between the *hollow* of his palms, he stretches them up and prays to Olódùmarè, offering the kola-nut; then he casts the valves within the circle. Often a *white fowl* is offered in the same way.[1]

The "circle" in the above quotation can stand not only for eternity but also for the ring of the sky and thus safely define Olódùmarè as a sky god. Let us, however, take a closer look at the semiotic context in which worship is offered to him, following the italicized highlights we made in the quoted passage.

1. The circle of eternity/sky ring which designates Olódùmarè is drawn using "ashes or white chalk." The color of both is white. This color is commonly associated with completeness but also with death and nonbeing. Besides, ash is a product of combustion, i.e. annihilation. Such a chain of references to mortality is suggestive. The circle made by the Olódùmarè worshiper may imply the idea of eternity but it may also point to the consideration that the surest gateway to that eternity is death.

2. The water used in the ritual is cold. Coldness is another attribute of death. Unlike the "water of life" (traditional name for wine or distilled alcohol) which tastes "hot" and is used in many other rituals (including many African ones), this water does not seem to suggest any vital power; it invites meditation, rather than ecstasy.

3. The cotton wool which the worshiper places his offering on is also white and suggestive of nonbeing and disappearance.

4. The offering is surrounded by emptiness, "the hollow of his palms," which can also be interpreted as nonbeing that enshrouds a material object.

5. A white fowl can be offered as part of the same ritual. The color of that fowl does not need any further comment.

Thus we can see that almost everything in the above ritual suggests the idea of transcendency, immateriality, elatedness but also, by extension, that of absence, nonbeing, and death. The symbol seems to deny itself, to transform itself into a blank and to erase the sign, leaving only a weak imprint.

1. Idowu, *Olódùmarè*, p. 142, emphasis added in all instances.

The above observation is congruent with the myth which Idowu tells in relation to what he styles Olódùmarè's "attributes."² In that myth:

> . . .it is Olódùmarè Himself who is represented as desiring immortality and seeking the guidance of the oracle. The oracle declared that what He sought was attainable; but He must offer a sacrifice and perform a certain rite. The main part of the rite was that He should rub His head with bar-wood dust. He did that; his head became exceedingly white and he became immortal.

Here again immortality is achieved by assuming the color of nonbeing. By whitening himself with bar-wood dust, Olódùmarè makes himself into an invisible spot and takes one step closer to becoming indiscernible in the thickening twilight of the gods.

Case Study 4. Nyame

We shall conclude our sketch on the sky god semiotics with a more detailed study of the chief deity in the Akan traditional religion—Nyame. He is possibly the best-known deity of West Africa and has a long tradition of theological and anthropological interpretations some of which we are going to use in our semiotic analysis below.

"Nyame" is only one of the names by which this deity is referred to. He is also widely known as Nyankopon and Odomankoma. Yet the name of choice is actually unimportant, for, as a contemporary author writes, this is not God's proper name but only an attributive designation:

> The Akans believe in One Eternal Invisible Spirit (Deity) that has no name or form. That is to say, that He answers to all names and is present in all forms. There is no representation of the Akan Deity as a form, either as an idol or as a portrait or painting.³

The above quote shows very clearly that the God of the Akan religion at its current stage of evolution has preserved almost no means of signification and is largely perceived as an inexpressible mystic entity. He is equally transcendent ("has no name or form") and immanent to this world ("answers to all names," i.e. can identified with any object of the phenomenal world which reveals his hidden omnipresence). Of course, Nyame, like any other ancient deity, has a whole cycle of creation myths associated with his name,

---

2. Idowu, *Olódùmarè*, p. 44.
3. Bempah, *Akan Traditional Religion*, 31.

where he displays a lot of anthropomorphic features and is far from being omniscient (cf. e.g., the stories where He is repeatedly tricked by Kwaku Anansi). However, this is no longer the prevailing notion of his divine nature at the topmost stage of generalization which the Akan religion has reached.

It is equally true that Nyame cannot be represented "either as an idol or as a portrait or painting." There seems to be only one extant way of representing him still available—the ideographic one which can be found in the famous book by R.S. Rattray (1881–1938) who reports having seen altars erected to Nyame all over the Ashanti Kingdom. He gives a short description of a representative altar accompanied by a page-size photograph:

> But it is hardly an exaggeration to say that every compound in Ashanti contains an altar to the Sky God, in the shape of a forked branch cut from a certain tree [. . .] which the Ashanti call '*Nyame dua*, lit. God's tree. Between the branches, which are cut short, is placed a basin, or perhaps a pot, and in this receptacle is generally to be found (besides the offering) a Neolithic celt ('*Nyame akuma*, God's axe).[4]

The symbol of the sky god as described and illustrated by Rattray looks very appropriate for the Supreme Being. It rests on three props whose number may imply the idea of infinity on the one hand (three dots defining an infinite plane) and that of stability on the other hand (based on the physical stability of any structure with three bearing points). The sink that stands at the top is simply the reverse image of the firmament which is often compared with an overturned cup. Finally, the Neolithic celt to be found inside is a perfect example of a quasi-natural symbol similar to round stones, crooked sticks or scrap motorcycle parts that we noted when we talked about the Fall of Man.

It is remarkable, however, that Rattray seems to be the last person to have spotted those altars. No other author after him (and none before him, by the way) knows about such structures or people making offerings to them. Yet we should not be surprised at this evasiveness of the Nyame cult, bearing in mind the process of continuous withdrawal and loss of signification which this deity has been undergoing ever since the day when He took offense with the fufu-pounding woman. What was still thought suitable for representation of Nyame yesterday may be judged to be too "idolatrous" or "fetishist" today. No wonder then that no one can nowadays observe the altars which must have formerly adorned "every compound in Ashanti."

The only visible sign of the Supreme Being which can still be observed today among the Akan is their famous Adinkra symbols ("Adinkira" in

4. Rattray, *Ashanti*, 142.

Rattray's spelling). Originally only stamped on cloth to be used for dressing up at funerals, they are now becoming more and more widespread as a very special sign of cultural self-identification among the Akan, spreading also to their neighboring peoples (Ewe, for example). The origin of those symbols is lost in the darkness of the past. Some of them look transparent enough in respect of the relation of form to meaning, while others seem almost impenetrable. I should like to concentrate on two of them that relate to Nyame: no. 18 and no. 35 respectively in Rattray's table.[5] I deliberately omit the most famous one—no. 37 *Gye Nyame*—"Except God (I fear none)"—because I find it too complicated to allow any brief analysis. In my view, this symbol is a kind of modified swastika—and to research all the aspects of its provenance and functioning would probably require a separate study other than this book. The other two signs I am going to analyze are nevertheless quite illuminating in their own right.

Figure 3. Gye Nyame Symbol

No. 18 represents the already familiar "altar to the Sky God"—*Nyame dua*. Unlike, the actual altar, it is neither triangular nor circular in shape but looks like an elaborate cross with rounded edges split in two and turned inside the figure. Where the split ends meet, they form four small internal crosses which point to the center of the main cross. This is quite appropriate for a structure which is not designed to stand erect but to stick to the flat surface of cloth. The cross is, of course, not an exclusively Christian symbol. It is extremely polysemic and in this example probably stands for the four points of the compass, i.e. once again serves to express the idea of omnitude and infinity. The altar is also the point where heaven and earth, humanity and divinity, cross each other. The plurality of small crosses can be said, therefore, to match with the singularity of the heavenly cross. The rounded

---

5. See Rattray, *Religion and Art in Ashanti*, 266–267.

edges may simply represent clouds or stand for incomplete circles of humanity, which, once again, can be opposed to the summary completeness of divinity that the figure ultimately represents.

Figure 4. Nyame dua Symbol

When we turn next to no. 35, we can simply regard it as the previous figure which has undergone radical simplification. It is called *Nyame nwu na ma wu*—"May Nyame die before I die." The figure retains the shape of a cross but its previously split ends have now become almost regular circles. The disappearance of internal circles is remarkable—man is no longer opposed to God or views himself as God's inferior but tries to combine the two infinities (the cross and the circle) in the expression of mystic identity. One cannot help noticing at the same time that the immortality of man is purchased in this case at the cost of God's becoming mortal or at least allowing for God's potential mortality. This is very characteristic of Akan culture, being the subject of a famous proverb which has puzzled generations of researchers by its apparently pessimistic and even Nietzschean undertones: "Odomankoma (another name for God) created Death and Death killed him."

Figure 5. Nyame nwu na ma wu Symbol

Death in this context can be simply viewed as a next-generation god, similar to what we observe in Greek mythology where Cronus overthrows his father Uranus only to be in turn overthrown by his son Zeus. Indeed, there are reasons to suppose that Nyame Himself did not belong to the first generation and probably started his career as a day-god—considering that Akan tradition says that He was born on Saturday. Like Jupiter, he might have one day risen from day-god to Supreme Being but then, like Saturn, he might have been downgraded to day-god again by someone begotten by him who later proved stronger than him.

Alternatively, as we saw in the paradox of Olódùmarè, death can be treated as a symbolic attribute of immortality. One cannot help remembering in this connection the famous saying attributed to Thales of Miletus (c. 624/623—c. 548/545 BC) one of the Seven Sages of Ancient Greece. This particular thinker among other things claimed that "there was no difference between life and death."[6]

On a still more sophisticated level, we can say that the sky god progresses to a more advanced representation of himself. While the original Nyame still retains, as we have noted above, some anthropomorphic features from the creation myth, he subsequently appears under a more generalized and almost featureless image—an impersonal force without any past or background. The death of Odomankoma can be thus interpreted as just another step towards God shedding his signification, a further stride towards the twilight of mysticism.

It remains to be added, however, that since approximately the middle of the twentieth century this progression towards disappearance has been pointedly slowed down and, in some instances, even reversed. This is mostly due to the two main factors:

1. The use of "Nyame" in the Twi translation of the Bible. As a result, the serene Akan God, who was used to withholding his reserve powers only for extraordinary events, had to adopt the unusual role of the Jewish "jealous God" who tended to meticulously monitor even minor transgressions of the people He patronizes. We shall talk a little bit more about that type of god in the next chapter.

2. The appearance of several "defenders of faith" who tried to prove that the African God differed from the God of Abrahamic religions in name only. *The Akan Doctrine of God* by J.B. Danquah (1895–1965) was a pioneering project in that field. However, facing the absence of any organized cult (writing 20 years after Rattray) and dismissing all other deities as "nothing else but superstition"[7] that author was left

---

6. As reported by Diogenes Laërtius (third century AD) in *Lives and Opinions of Eminent Philosophers*, §19.

7. Danquah, *The Akan Doctrine of God*, 91.

with little else but etymologies of God's various names which he, after much reshuffling, stacked into a semblance of the Christian Trinity. After this exercise, Nyame certainly gained in importance, even though that gain had to be compensated by increased responsibility for things usually delegated to minor powers. Being thus rather artificially inflated, Nyame has cut only a poor figure in comparison with the well-established Christian God who has a long history and rich cult behind him. It is quite possible that Danquah's undertaking only precipitated the decline of the Akan traditional religion already underway at the time of expounding his *doctrine*.

Chapter XI

Lighting the Twilight: Renewal vs Denial

THERE ARE TWO ESSENTIAL ways of response to the perceived twilight of the gods which we can conventionally style as *renewal* and *denial*.

Renewal usually means the advent of a new-generation god. This change of generations may or may not be accompanied by a change of orientation, e.g., when the main thrust of devotion is redirected from the sky god to the earth goddess, from a zoomorphic to an anthropomorphic deity etc. Very often, to avoid the fate of his predecessors who tended to withdraw from active involvement in human affairs once the creation was completed, the new god shows greater interest man's day-to-day life. Hence Zeus's persistent efforts at impregnating the largest possible number among womankind or YHWH's micromanagement of his chosen people. The new god often procures some attributes to ensure his greater visibility (lightning, pillar of cloud/fire) which he may do by merging with a member of his retinue. Every deity, sooner or later, falls victim to "overexposure," becoming less and less noticeable. However, as we pointed out in the previous chapter, the existence/emergence of written tradition can considerably slow down or even reverse that process.

God the Son in Christianity certainly belongs to this "new generation" category. Yet, because so many people believe him to be the only true God, he deserves a special chapter. Right now, we should rather concentrate on the second option of reacting to the twilight of the gods which consists in refusing to renew the current covenants or to replace it with a new one. The alternative to renewal is *atheism*. It arises whenever one finds it impossible or inexpedient to resupply or restore the worn-out means of signification and tries to replace them with a *zero sign* instead. This is the best that man can do in expressing the idea of nonbeing which can only be perceived as *absence*, as negative existence and not as a neutral "void."

This is a trap into which every atheist is doomed to fall—the impossibility to signify the non-existence of something or someone in any other way than *to negate a certain symbol by using another symbol*. As soon as such a zero sign is introduced, we trigger the millennia-old mechanism which stipulates that there is no signifier without a signified. God, even if his non-existence is postulated, remains a powerful sign which encapsulates the inertia of all human culture. As we try to argue below, this force is virtually impossible to withstand.

One may question the expediency of discussing atheism in a book on African religion. Indeed, atheism plays only a marginal role in the life of that continent. However, without a proper understanding of the semiotic nature of this cultural phenomenon our picture of religion would be incomplete. Besides, Africa is certainly not immune to the problem. Atheism may still be deemed socially unacceptable or even punishable by law in many parts of Africa but one can hardly be as certain at the individual level. African atheism is certainly going to grow in importance with the spread of Western secular education and Western-type consumerist ideology. Yet, because it is still far from attaining full maturity and exists in Africa only in the form of provocative statements of several high-brow intellectuals (Wole Soyinka etc.) I prefer to use a western sample for our analysis, and I choose for that purpose probably the best-known book of our days written on the subject –*The God Delusion* by Richard Dawkins (first published in 2008).

What makes that book a rewarding object of study is the fact that its author has a marked propensity to express himself in symbolic forms which he usually borrows from his main field of occupation—evolutionary biology. By doing so, he often unknowingly reveals some controversial "seams" and "joints" of his theoretical construct—something that a professional philosopher or theologian would be cautious enough to hide. In other words, *The God Delusion* can serve as a good illustration to the semiotics of atheism. A close look at the author's idiom may tell us a lot about the actual contents of his message.

Anyone who has at least some familiarity with the works of Richard Dawkins would know how metaphorical his style tends to be. The title of his very first book—*The Selfish Gene* (the book I value very highly, as I am going to show in chapter XIV)—is a good case in point. The gene has, of course, no consciousness and cannot be attributed any human feelings, including selfishness. The author is perfectly aware of this circumstance and repeatedly issues apologies and caveats to that effect. He tirelessly reiterates, over and over again, that such a manner of presentation is not, strictly speaking, correct, but is used nevertheless throughout the book for the sake of convenience. But what is that convenience?

First, it saves space; second, it touches the strings of our cultural memory (our "memes" as Dawkins himself would say), which would otherwise remain unaffected, and thus makes our intake of information more "organic," i.e. more efficient than by purely rational means. This manner of expression is certainly not Dawkins's invention but simply an elaboration on our habitual way of expressing ourselves. Thus, it is a well-known linguistic fact that when we speak, for example, about the sun, we typically say that it "rises" even though we are aware nowadays that we refer thereby only to a visual impression (indeed, a *delusion*) which results from our observing the changing position of the earth in relation to the sun, *from* the earth. Yet we prefer to use an expression which derives from our animistic past and which implies that the earth, being the most important body of the universe, remains fixed in the center, while the sun, its "servant," obediently moves around, compelled in its motion by the sense of duty and fear of disobedience. Like all other living beings, it has to rise in the morning and get to work. While doing so, it must obey the rules set by the general order of the universe. As the famous fragment from Heraclitus of Ephesus (c. 535—c. 475 BC) says, "The sun will not overstep his measures; if he does, the Erinyes, the handmaids of Justice, will find him out" (Burnet 94).

There are good reasons for us to do so. To express the same thing in a "non-animistic" fashion, we would need a considerably greater number of words. We would have to say something like "The sun, on account of the earth's rotation around it, has become visible at the longitude where we are now located by gradually moving in the direction perpendicular to the line that marks the limit of visibility (commonly known as 'the horizon') until it finally came in full view for the earthly observer."

I did my best in the previous paragraph to avoid using the dangerously metaphoric verb "to rise." This resulted in a very confusing sentence which has absolutely no appeal to our intuitive perception of habitual things around us. Our whole cultural experience teaches us that the sun rises in the morning in order to pursue its daily chores, similarly to other animals and human beings. This holds basically true for many other statements. In most cases, it is much easier to describe a natural phenomenon as if it were performed by a conscious individual prompted by some internal or external compulsion. The same applies to God when it comes to expressing the most generalized notions. Let us take, for example, such an apparently "innocent" phrase "Only God knows what it is really like" and try to translate it into non-metaphoric language. We obviously cannot simply replace it with the sentence "Nobody knows what it actually is" because the original phrase implies a fact whose causes are unknown to us at the moment but, nonetheless, exist in objective reality and can therefore become known to us in the fullness of time, and can now only be presumed to be known to their hypothetical creator or omniscient observer commonly referred to as "God." I hope the above examples make it clear why Richard Dawkins prefers metaphorical idiom in presenting his ideas, even though, as we shall soon see, this means of expression can easily backfire.

Thus, one of the central metaphors around which the author of *The God Delusion* builds his argumentation is the opposition of two lifting devices: the *crane* and the *skyhook*. The former stands for Darwin's evolutionary theory, the latter for religious metaphysics. The author keeps on claiming that the "crane" provides a more convincing explanation of the mechanism which underlies all processes of development in the universe. This supposedly vivid image is persistently used throughout the book, which feels almost like an endless repetition:[1]

> They [the extraterrestrial creatures believed by some people to determine our earthly fortunes] probably owe their existence to a (perhaps unfamiliar) version of Darwinian evolution: some sort of cumulatively ratcheting 'crane' as opposed to 'skyhook' [. . .] Skyhooks—including all gods—are magic spells. They do no bona fide explanatory work and demand more explanation than they provide. Cranes are explanatory devices that actually do explain.[2]

And again:

> We need a 'crane', not a 'skyhook', for only a crane can do the business of working up gradually and plausibly from simplicity to otherwise improbable complexity.
> 4. The most ingenious and powerful crane so far discovered is Darwinian evolution by natural selection.[3]

And again:

---

1. "Crane" is used 23 times and "skyhook" 6 times. The dichotomy is not Dawkins's own invention but, according to his own admission (*The God Delusion*, endnote 44) is borrowed by him from *Darwin's Dangerous Idea* (1995) by Daniel Dennett.
2. Dawkins, *The God Delusion*, 99.
3. Dawkins, *The God Delusion*, 188.

> We should not give up hope of a better crane arising in physics, something as powerful as Darwinism is for biology. But even in the absence of a strongly satisfying crane to match the biological one, the relatively weak cranes we have at present are, when abetted by the anthropic principle, self-evidently better than the self-defeating skyhook hypothesis of an intelligent designer.[4]

The difference between the crane and the skyhook, as far as I understand it, is that the former is a self-sufficient mechanism—it does not require application of any outside force in order to operate; while the latter needs "a hand" from above—something or someone to provide external fixing point which the mechanism has to rely on in operation. Richard Dawkins seems to find this difference illustrative enough to have a substantial part of his argumentation rest on it. Yet the imagery he employs for that purpose is far from flawless. One may raise at least three objections with respect to its appropriateness:

1. Both the crane and the skyhook are products of *intelligent design* the idea of which the author vehemently denies throughout his book. Why use images so highly suggestive of intelligent design to disprove that idea? Besides, the crane as such is only relatively more self-sufficient. Just like the skyhook, it requires its own "Archimedean point"—in practice, usually four adjustable supports that form a plane for it to rest on. Why use such similar mechanisms to describe such conflicting notions? Are we not dealing with the same "sacred twin" archetype that we briefly mentioned the Introduction? If so, which of the two devices is "sacred"? For Dawkins it is most certainly his beloved Darwinian crane. But why? Is it only because the word "skyhook" has an annoyingly supernatural connotation due to the "sky" element in it and is bound for that reason to swap its primogeniture with the crane which looks to be more appropriate as a "nature-given" symbol because of its ornithological connotations (the *crane* is a bird species of the *Gruidae* family, rather than a manmade machine)? However, this "natural" symbol, by defeating its "supernatural" counterpart, can also easily inherit the latter's supernatural properties. By repeatedly extolling his intelligent crane and subverting the discredited skyhook Richard Dawkins only succeeds in creating a new (a highly fanciful one, we must admit) symbol of a supernatural creator. Obviously, this is very far from his intention but nevertheless a real impression that the reader can may derive from his discourse.

---

4. Dawkins, *The God Delusion*, 189.

2. The chain of associations can be easily continued. Thus, the only true difference between the crane and the skyhook is that the latter is a simpler mechanism. However, this factor makes the crane even less suitable for the role of central symbol of a godless universe, considering that elsewhere in his book Richard Dawkins—in opposition to Richard Swinburne—maintains that a system without God is necessarily simpler than the one with God. Yet, at least on the associative level, he chooses a more complicated image to express an allegedly simpler construct.

3. It is also hard to overlook the strong linkage that exists in Dawkins's mind between the image of the crane and that of Darwin. Apart from the passages cited above, I have counted five more occasions on which "crane" and "Darwin" (or its derivatives "Darwinian" and "Darwinism") stand together in the same sentence or in adjacent sentences. "Darwin's powerful crane" which occurs twice, is, in my opinion, the greatest hit of all. What result does this persistent pairing of "Darwin" with "crane" achieve? I cannot answer, of course, for all Dawkins's readers but what I picture in my mind as a result of this constant juxtaposition is a very tall crane whose tower reaches far into the sky and in whose cabin I discern *an old man with a long white beard* whose name is Charles Darwin. As we know from the book, the image of an old hoary man stands for a primitive idea of God, discarded by modern theists but allegedly still attributed to them by low-brow atheists. This reproach, according to Dawkins, cannot be taken seriously and serves no defense for the theists:

> That old man is an irrelevant distraction and his beard is as tedious as it is long. Indeed, the distraction is worse than irrelevant. Its very silliness is calculated to distract attention from the fact that what the speaker really believes is not a whole lot less silly[5].

Yet he recreates exactly the same image when he presents his own view of the way the universe is managed. Charles Darwin, the divine crane man . . . Why is Dawkins so careless in choosing his imagery in a book where every miscalculated step can expose him to the derision of his opponents? Or does he mean it? Does he really want to attribute divine features to his scientific idol? Is evolutionary theory the only true religion? Some passages of *The God Delusion* do invite such a reading. See, for example,

---

5. Dawkins, *The God Delusion*, 57.

what is required, according to Dawkins, to get a true understanding of how things run in this world:

> At an intellectual level, I suppose he [Fred Hoyle] understood natural selection. But perhaps you need to be steeped in natural selection, immersed in it, swim about in it, before you can truly appreciate its power.[6]

Once again, one must be really an all-forgiving Dawkins fan not to spot an obvious allusion to baptism is this passage. People who have gone through immersion in natural selection are the born-agains, the selected few, the initiates who truly inherit the kingdom. In Dawkins's parlance they are called people who "have had their consciousness raised by Darwin/natural selection" (pages 189 and 175 respectively). The others, the lost ones, are at the very best, "people with undifferentiated consciousness," although Richard Dawkins would probably object to using a term borrowed from a Catholic author, Bernard Lonergan[7] (1904–1984).

Do not take me wrong—I do not doubt the authenticity of Richard Dawkins's atheism, nor do I question the theoretical validity of atheism as such. I only wanted to show how difficult it is to profess one's atheism without subconsciously creating a kind of surrogate religion. This, as I have already said a few times, is down to our cultural background. The best we can hope to achieve in such circumstances is to present the image of an *absent* God, not a *non-existing* one. But in semiotic perspective, absence can be just as meaningful as presence. For example, absence of an indefinite article in front of a singular noun in English usually means that the noun belongs to the uncountable class—it does not cancel the existence of the article as a part of speech, nor its functions on occasions when it is present in front of the noun. A zero used within a number in mathematics does not mean that the number is inferior to another one where that sign is not used. A number multiplied by zero does not cease to exist.

The phrase "There is no God" has only a contextual, not an absolute, meaning in human language. The ontological argument for God's existence, although convincingly criticized by many thinkers, holds valid within the system of signification that has been in place since the dawn of humanity. Asserting the non-existence of God is like using some primitive software where every time we want to use a word in the desired meaning we have to manually switch from the default setting and where on every other occasion we use it the system automatically reverts back to the default, unless

---

6. Dawkins, *The God Delusion*, 142.
7. See *Method in Theology* (1971).

we change it manually again or, worse, restart the computer or, worse still, reformat the hard drive. Or, to use a more traditional set of values (which I, personally, am more accustomed to, considering my background, let us quote from Robert Browning's (1812–89) *Bishop Blougram's Apology*, where the same idea is expressed, in my opinion, in a brilliantly concise fashion:

> And now what are we? unbelievers both,
> Calm and complete, determinately fixed
> To-day, to-morrow and for ever, pray?
> You'll guarantee me that? Not so, I think!
> In no wise! all we've gained is, that belief,
> As unbelief before, shakes us by fits,
> Confounds us like its predecessor. Where's
> The gain? how can we guard our unbelief,
> Make it bear fruit to us?—the problem here.
> Just when we are safest, there's a sunset-touch,
> A fancy from a flower-bell, some one's death,
> A chorus-ending from Euripides,—
> And that's enough for fifty hopes and fears
> As old and new at once as nature's self,
> To rap and knock and enter in our soul,
> Shake hands and dance there, a fantastic ring,
> Round the ancient idol, on his base again,—
> The grand Perhaps! We look on helplessly.
> There the old misgivings, crooked questions are—
> This good God,—what he could do, if he would,
> Would, if he could . . .

What would we recommend to an atheist facing such a predicament? To reprogram our mental universe where the non-existence of God would serve as a central algorithm? Or perhaps to relocate into a parallel world whose basic settings would suit our godless preferences? Or, if that is impossible, maybe to build/design a universe where the sun would not rise but only display the visual effects of the earth's rotating around it? But how long would we carry on in such a world, considering that we have other humans to stay in touch with? But I have almost forgotten that my self-imposed role in this study is that of an observer, not an adviser.

Therefore, I shall limit myself to the following brief conclusion: Although we can probably, in Dawkins phrase, "kill religion"[8] by consistently pursuing the path of denial as outlined in this chapter, we cannot kill religious consciousness which has been hard-wired into our brains from the beginning. If someone wanted to accomplish the Dawkins mission, both

---

8. Dawkins, *The God Delusion*, 7.

language and technology would have to follow suite. Indeed, it is mostly into language and technology that the religious consciousness relocates with the decline of organized religion as witnessed by modern civilization. We shall return to the problem of this unity later, when we speak about "Progress vs Conservatism" in chapter XVII.

By the way, if you want my honest opinion, I find nothing wrong about the old man with a white beard. As such, this image stands for wisdom—which is one of God's chief attributes and probably the most adequate sign of his presence in the world which looks rational (=intelligent/wise) to us. There is no better way for a human being to visualize perfect wisdom than to imagine an old man with a grey beard. I only object to that beard being long—there can be nothing disproportionate in God. I do not understand, therefore, why modern theists so persistently disown this symbol which they apparently find to be a sign of backwardness.

I can also guess why so many famous thinkers and teachers of mankind who were active in the late nineteenth century were so fond of putting up the appearance of old men with long white beards—both Darwin and Tylor, for example, looked like that. It may be that with their propensity to lose sight of the theistic God they tried to compensate for that shortage by assuming the archetypal look of wisdom which they thus wanted to impersonate.

Enough about atheism, however. From now on, we shall speak no more about the denial option and concentrate on that of renewal. Doing this will hopefully let us answer another important question: What makes Christianity unique among other religions?

Chapter XII

The Christs of Africa

As we noted in the previous chapter, the figure of Jesus in Christianity fits, on the whole, the definition of a next-generation god. He is begotten by the creator God who then seems (if not dogmatically, at least practically) to withdraw to heaven and delegate to his son virtually all stewardship of the universe, including the actual completion of the divine plan concerning the making and management of the material world and all its inhabitants (John 1:3; 1 Cor 8:6). Being put in charge of mundane matters, the Son dutifully assumes the responsibilities of an earth god or, more specifically, the god of agriculture and viniculture as evidenced by his main attributes—bread and wine—identical with his body and blood. As a proper agricultural god he sacrifices himself for the benefit of mankind by allowing himself to be murdered and buried in order to rise again, being a symbolic representation of a crop whose seeds must die in order to revive later (1 Cor 15:36) and ensure sustenance for the people—his worshipers.

Personalities like this and stories associated with them abound in religions all over the world, including Africa. I find the Yoruba religion particularly striking in that respect and I want once more (and for the last time—I promise) to turn for an example to Idowu's brilliant study (*Olódùmarè*) which does not seem to lose topicality in this fast-changing world.

Unlike Christianity, the Yoruba religion does not invest the idea of the earth god in a single deity but distributes it among several personages. The actual distribution of functions and the number of deities that receive corresponding attributes may vary depending on the region, place of worship, school of thought, prevailing occupation of the local population etc. However, the most obvious candidate for a Christ-figure, at least as it appears from reading Idowu, seems to be the "arch-divinity" called Orisa (which, as the author claims, was initially the name of a single god before it got "diffused" into multiple deities and became a common name). This original Orisa "descended into the world to fulfil the functions allotted"[1] to him by Olódùmarè. As a true agricultural god, he was given the ownership of the whole land, a small part of which he rented out to his slave Atowoda. The latter was supposed to act as Orisa's tenant, cultivating the land and rendering account on his activities to his master. Those who recollect the Parable of the Wicked Tenants (Matt 21:33–41) can now easily guess what happened next. The ungrateful slave, in striking parallel with the gospel story, decided to plot against his master and eventually arranged his death. He procured a large round stone and when Orisa came to pay an inspector's visit to the farm, everything was ready to perform this sacrifice-disguised-as-murder:[2]

> From the top of the hill, Atowoda watched him—his *habitual white clothing* marked him out clearly. When Atowoda was sure that there could be no escape for him, he suddenly gave the stone a push; the stone made straight for the arch-divinity; the arch-divinity, *paralysed with astonishment and terror*, could not escape; he was *crushed to bits and scattered*.[3]

At least three things are worth noting in the quoted passage: 1) The white clothing of Orunmila contributes to his death—much in the same way as we saw the color white being ominous for Olódùmarè in the "Twilight" chapter. This circumstance suggests Orunmila's "consubstantiality" with his heavenly father. 2) Orunmila's immobility while watching the deadly stone approach him is only poorly explained by his "astonishment and terror." Can an arch-divinity succumb to such feelings? It may have looked like that for Atowoda but for us it is a piece of circumstantial evidence to suggest that Orunmila was accepting his death voluntarily, as a necessary sacrifice for the benefit of humanity. 3) Orunmila's body is "crushed to bits and scattered" by a large stone. This stone, which at first sight appears simply as a murder weapon, at closer look evokes associations with either a grinding or a threshing appliance. The use of both of them results in breaking (=scattering) the divine body of a crop which is supposed to revive afterwards "more abundantly" (John 10:10) either as food or as newly sprouted grain. The same type of transformation is reproduced, albeit in a different setting, in

1. Idowu, *Olódùmarè*, 59.
2. See the "Blood as Spiritual Currency" chapter for other examples.
3. Idowu, *Olódùmarè*, 59, emphasis added.

the act of Jesus breaking bread identified with his own body (1 Cor 11:24) and which is intended to be distributed (=scattered) among his present and future disciples as part of communion service.

A very similar thing happens to Orisa. His companion god Orunmila soon learns about this tragic incident. As soon as he did so:

> He performed a certain rite which made it possible for him to find all the scattered pieces. These he collected in a calabash [. . .] There he deposited a portion of the pieces and then distributed the rest "all over the world."[4]

It is remarkable that Orunmila manages to gather all the pieces of Orisa's scattered flesh in a calabash—a vessel usually used to store liquid. Perhaps it was the arch-divinity's blood he originally collected. Besides, the size of calabash is hardly enough to take in the whole of Orisa's dismembered body. Whatever it was, blood or flesh, Orunmila's part in this story is strikingly similar to that of Joseph of Arimathea, while his calabash assumes the role resembling that of the Holy Grail. As for Orisa himself, his flesh is distributed all over the world as becomes any other agricultural god promoting his crop. The same happens to Jesus whose body/bread and blood/wine are capable of satisfying a permanently expanding number of his worshipers worldwide.

I said at the beginning of this chapter that some functions that Christ combines in one person can be distributed among several African deities. Thus, while Orisa in the example above clearly shows certain features of a self-sacrificing god, his resurrection can be assumed only if we know about the existence of stories where this event is more pronounced (e.g., those of Osiris, Dionysus or Jesus). This is because in Yoruba religion there is a specialized deity to express that idea. His name is Sango and the myth associated with him contains the famous exclamation "The King did not hang himself!"[5] This is because his followers believe that, whatever his motives were, he did not commit suicide but ascended to heaven. The story bears obvious resemblance to the news of Jesus having conquered death that originally spread among the narrow cycle of his disciples but gradually acquired an ever-increasing number of believers. We can thus say that in the case of Yoruba religion two deities, Orisa and Sango, jointly provide for the complex symbol which in Christianity is expressed in Jesus alone.

Nevertheless, in the examples above, the differences between the role of Jesus in Christianity and those of Orisa and Sango in Yoruba religion are not essential and can be brought to a common denominator using the

---

4. Idowu, *Olódùmarè*, 60.
5. Idowu, *Olódùmarè*, 90.

grid proposed by Claude Lévy-Strauss (1908–2009) for the collection and collation of myths that belong to the same cycle.[6] One has to admit that it is impossible to tell what makes Christianity unique among other religions if we restrict ourselves only to the legendary biographies of their founders. Whenever we attempt a comparison, we shall only find variations in the settings of the same archetypal situation—change of divine generations, renewal of divine signification. This inconvenient truth has been vividly acknowledged by Hans Urs von Balthasar (1905–1988) who was writing in the aftermath of the Second Vatican Council—the time when the Catholic Church had, probably for the first time, decided to address the complexities of ecumenism and religious pluralism in earnest. For him, to claim that Christianity is the only true religion would be the same as:

> . . . to assert that one wave in the river that has flowed on for millions of years and will continue to flow on unthinkable for yet more millions once the wave is no more, can be identified with the river. Nonsense, too, to assert that this wave has already comprehended all that future and enclosed within itself the fulness of time and the end of time. On attempting to estimate the degree of provocation in such fantastic claims, we see clearly that any school of religious or philosophic thought must be surprised and further shocked by another statement in the same context: "They hated me without cause" (John 15:25).[7]

Balthasar was brave enough to pose the question but lacked courage to give a meaningful answer, for, later in the quoted article, he merely evades the issue by stating that the fact of Jesus' resurrection makes him stand out among the founders of other religions. By saying so he simply resorts to fideism, as, being an accomplished scholar, he could hardly be unaware of many other resurrecting gods who performed and occasionally still continue to perform their roles of nature renovators to the same, if not a better, effect. Yet there is something else to Jesus than his mythical biography, something that makes him rather unique in comparison with other proponents of religious renewal, including the African ones. This something is the existence of *written law* which underlie Jesus' way of thinking and teaching. It is his relationship with the Jewish Law that ultimately determines his fate and his influence on all subsequent development of religious views and practices.

6. See the respective chapter (11) in *Structural Anthropology*. I am also aware of a passionate denial of the very existence of that myth by Akinwumi Işola—see "Religious Politics and the Myth of Şango" in *African Traditional Religions in Contemporary Society*, 93–109, but I am afraid that this very denial can be fitted as a variation of the myth within Levy-Strauss's flexible grid.

7. Hans Urs von Balthasar, "Why I am still a Christian" in *Two Say Why*, 18.

Chapter XIII

The Semiotic Message of Jesus

INDEED, FOR JESUS, AS for any orthodox Jew, it is the written law, not the phenomenal world, that acts as the primary source of both transcendental truth and moral guidance. For him (as, in fact, nineteen centuries later also for Derrida, a person of Jewish background) the written word takes absolute priority both over the spoken one and over the sensually experienced reality. If that reality comes into apparent conflict with the Law, it is not the Law that is to blame but our imperfect reading of it, a deficiency of our vision, that prevents us from making out all its intricate shapes and shades. Ultimately, if the phenomenal world cannot assure an adequate representation of the law, it has to be discarded and replaced with a new creation—the Kingdom of God—whose semiotic properties will answer the purpose better. But until that happens, the written law must continue to predetermine our interaction with the material world:

> Think not that I am come to destroy the law, or the prophets: I am not come to destroy, but to fulfil. For verily I say unto you, Till heaven and earth pass, one jot or one tittle shall in no wise pass from the law, till all be fulfilled. Whosoever therefore shall break one of these least commandments, and shall teach men so, he shall be called the least in the kingdom of heaven: but whosoever shall do and teach them, the same shall be called great in the kingdom of heaven. (Matt 5:17–18)

What is remarkable in the above passage is the way that Jesus envisages the Law: not as a collection of rules but as an agglomeration of graphic symbols—jots and tittles—whose set combination must be preserved intact and passed on to future generations. It is from these elementary particles that the Law is expected to recreate itself under changing conditions without compromising its original integrity.

It is the same basic symbols into which we must, according to Jesus, analyze things manifested to our senses in order to assure the correct reading of our surroundings—by identifying the divine signs inscribed on them. This approach predominates in many of his sayings. The Parable of the Mustard Seed is a good example of that technique:

> The kingdom of heaven is like to a grain of mustard seed, which a man took, and sowed in his field: Which indeed is the least of all seeds: but when it is grown, it is the greatest among herbs, and becometh a tree, so that the birds of the air come and lodge in the branches thereof. (Mark 4:30–34; also in Matt 13:31–32 and Luke 13:18–19)

The "least of all seeds" acts as the most elementary sign. It looks almost like a geometrical abstraction—a sizeless point—that stands for a notion that has been conceived but not yet developed. Yet this point of conception is already suggestive of its entelechy (a beginning that contains its own end). The seed becomes a tree, a living organism in symbiosis with other creatures—an image of completeness and harmony.

The same approach to the reality can be traced in some of Jesus' miracles, especially those where the evangelists grudgingly reveal his actual healing techniques. An example of this kind can be found in the Gospel of Mark (8:22–26) where the healing session is described with unusual detail[1] and contains a remarkable interim stage:

> And he cometh to Bethsaida; and they bring a blind man unto him, and besought him to touch him. And he took the blind man by the hand, and led him out of the town; and when he had spit on his eyes, and put his hands upon him, he asked him if he saw ought. And he looked up, and said, I see men as trees, walking. After that he put his hands again upon his eyes, and made him look up: and he was restored, and saw every man clearly.

The healing here is effected in two steps. The blind man recovers his eyesight gradually. What he sees first is not a fully realistic picture but a

---

1. Another chance to learn a little bit more about Jesus' healing methods comes up in the Gospel of John (9:6) where, to treat another blind man, Jesus makes "clay of the spittle" which he applies to his patient's eyes. This Gospel, although quite advanced on its theology, can be often very conservative when it comes to reproducing the settings of events it describes.

symbolic representation of the reality—people looking like trees. As in the previous example, the tree acts here as a hieroglyphic image of any living individual. A simplistically depicted (and ideally also inverted) tree can be regarded as especially suitable for this function. Seeing symbols instead of real objects is very appropriate for someone whose eyesight of at an interim stage of recovery. The way to "seeing clearly" is through learning first to recognize the semiotic charge of surrounding objects which can only later be translated into direct projections of the image on the mind.

In other words, the surrounding reality must be first encoded before it can be meaningfully perceived. Although the above example is exceptional, we can still say that most of Jesus' parables and quite a few of his miracles are nothing else but attempts to engage his listeners in an independent search for those basic symbols which can be used to decode things around them. In the end, this decoding must result in assuring the visibility and, eventually, presence of the divine Kingdom on earth. This is the ultimate message that Jesus' wants to get across. This is evident from the fact that in most cases he refuses to explain the meaning of his parables to mass audience which he expects to make conscious efforts towards their own interpretation.

Jesus reaches only a moderate success in his attempts to awaken the semiotic skills of his listeners—both literate and illiterate ones. The former—Pharisees and scribes—find his reading of the Law too audacious and unorthodox to be acceptable for their legalistic stand. What Jesus claims to do in fulfilment of the Law, to them often looks more like destroying it. This difference in approaches becomes especially evident, for example, in their respective attitudes to the Sabbath. When Jesus performs some of his healings on Saturday, he asserts that such acts are perfectly appropriate because they only serve to emphasize the holiness of the day on which they are committed. A selfless deed for which no reward is demanded (and it was never reported that Jesus charged leech fees from his patients) does not constitute "work" and certainly cannot desecrate the Sabbath—just as non-observance of a fast (another form of abstention on religious grounds) cannot defile a person whose thoughts and acts manifest his internal purity (Matt 15:11).

The Pharisees and scribes, however, refuse to read such acts figuratively. They view the problem in terms of a simple binary opposition between occupation and rest. The most they can allow with respect to deviation from the Law is to treat such cases casuistically—as an exception to the rule or rather as an accidence to which the rule does not apply. Jesus subjects this position to ridicule because he finds it untenable:

> *Thou* hypocrite, doth not each one of you on the sabbath loose his ox or his ass from the stall, and lead *him* away to watering?

> So ought not this woman, being a daughter of Abraham, whom
> Satan hath bound, lo, these eighteen years, be loosed from this
> bond on the sabbath day? (Luke 13:15–16)
> Then He answered them, saying, "Which of you, having a donkey or an ox that has fallen into a pit, will not immediately pull him out on the Sabbath day?" (Luke 14:5)

Too many exceptions, according to Jesus, will simply invalidate the rule. In a situation like that he insists on the figurative reading of the rule as the only feasible one. Although originating from the same school of thought, the two viewpoints seem irreconcilable (at least in the way they are presented in the Gospel). The literate camp, which counts many influential people, finally turns against Jesus and to a great extent contributes to his arrest.

As for the illiterate part of Jesus' audience, which includes some of his best disciples (the fishermen Peter, James, and John among them) and certainly all his female followers, they could be expected to be more susceptible to his teaching, being not bound by the shackles of written law. Yet their misinterpretation (we cannot say "misreading" in this case) of the Master can be no less serious for that. To begin with, they always press him to reveal the hidden meaning of his parables—something he refuses to do for the mass audience. He reluctantly yields to their demands but this concession seems to run contrary to his original intention—to have his listeners work out the moral of his stories independently. He keeps on explaining his sayings even when he possibly thinks it is time that his disciples started composing their own parables (which they never learn to do, by the way).

Jesus' illiterate audience seems highly unwilling to develop independent judgement. It is only human, after all, to expect ready-made solutions, rather than have them presented in the do-it-yourself packaging. Instead of accepting their teacher as an intermediary figure that only assists in comprehending the truth, they start to treat him as the first-hand source of that truth, as a universal reference point which alone is capable to tell the right bearings for everyone who wants to find his way through the world. Finally, he is perceived as an impersonation of the absolute truth.

Seeing all this, Jesus looks extremely worried that he may thus fail his earthly mission. He knows that his time is short and that his simmering conflict with the authorities can escalate at any time, causing his premature departure from this world. He repeatedly raises this subject in conversations with his disciples, trying to make them realize this pending inevitability (Matt 16:21; Luke 17:25 etc.). He succeeds, however, only in further convincing them in his prophetic qualities, so much that one of his favorite disciples (Peter) finally professes him as the Messiah (Matt 16:16).

At this point Jesus probably gives up his attempts to get across with his semiotic message. He does not rebuke Peter for his "discovery" although he does prohibit to publicize it, at least for the time being. Perhaps, to position himself as the sole bearer of truth is the only way to teach the right things to these people. Jesus seems to put up with the messianic role imposed on him by his followers. He stops talking in parables. He becomes a very different Jesus—the Jesus of the Gospel of John, rather than the synoptic gospels. He knows that his end is near but he also hopes that the jots and tittles of the old law will become the seeds and cuttings that will grow into trees whose roots will be firmly implanted in earth, while their leaves will reach heaven.

When the news about Jesus' resurrection begins to spread quickly among his followers (whose number would grow exponentially over the next century) his transformation into the universal symbol becomes more and more complete. The establishment of that symbol makes all other symbols redundant. This idea finds its full expression in the Pauline epistles. Paul of Tarsus, who never knew Jesus in his human capacity but only in his divine hypostasis, is simply not interested in the master's personality, not even in his teaching. He only cares for the reality of his resurrection, and not just resurrection as such but only in relation to the redemption of the original sin. Because Jesus was dead but now is alive, the Law itself can be declared dead.

The only use that Paul still reserves for the defunct Law is to provide a "library" of non-binding references whose only function is to highlight the absoluteness of the Christ symbol through their own relativity. Paul thus does not aim at destroying the Law but only at disabling its "control center." The idea of redemption through observing a certain set of rules now gives way to redemption through believing in a single miraculous event, i.e. salvation by faith. Having made this replacement, he is now free to manipulate the whole corpus of the Law by recombining, allegorizing, reinterpreting, and in any other ways rearranging its signs and images to fit his new message.

Paul tries to use the same approach when he comes across a non-Abrahamic tradition and outlines the way it could be assimilated by Christianity. The above described "replacement" technique is clearly visible in his speech before the Areopagus. Whatever the historicity of the Book of Acts (17:22–34) which relates this episode in Paul's career, one thing is certain: its author demonstrates good knowledge of the apostle's rhetorical skills.

Paul starts by choosing a single reference point. In this case, it is THE UNKNOWN GOD which he believes to be worshipped by the Athenians. He clearly senses an obvious opportunity: an unknown god is a vacant symbol that can assume any contents and as such may stand either for everything or nothing. Paul's objective is to change from naught to one, transform the message from negative into affirmative, highlight a previously neglected entity and then let it expand over the whole of religious consciousness. When he assumes that he has succeeded in this task—that he has disabled the control center of pagan religion—he immediately appeals to its written tradition, to the library of its symbolic forms which he thinks he can now manipulate at his discretion.

Certainly, Paul feels much less at home in Greek literature than he does in the Jewish religious writings. Nevertheless, he manages to provide a relevant quotation from as many as two poets (both in verse 28). He is not put off by the fact that one of those quotations paints God in rather panentheistic colors ("For in him we live, and move, and have our being"), while the other one tends to represent God rather as a pagan ancestor than Abrahamic creator ("as certain also of your own poets have said, For we are also his offspring"). The principle of divine procreation, being assigned its proper "shelf" in Paul's library of symbols, can now be reinterpreted metaphorically—as a synonymous expression for God the Maker-of-Everything. And all this because, according to Paul, there can be only one non-metaphoric expression of divinity—that of Christ risen from the dead.

Paul's speech, although quite short, sounds quite cogent. It fails to convince most of his audience not because of his lack of logic but because of what I think to be the incorrect choice of the initial reference point. The idea of an unknown god was certainly very marginal for Greek religion. Just as marginal are the poets he quotes in his sermon. Had Paul chosen to start with a Platonic definition of God and borrow his supporting metaphors from Homer, he would have definitely sounded more impressive to his listeners. His knowledge of Greek culture was, however, probably unfit for the occasion to assure his success. He certainly succeeded upon many other occasions—very likely because he was thenceforth more careful in his choice of starting points.

Let us now try to answer the question we have already asked a couple of times in this book: What makes Christianity unique? It is certainly not the contents of its message which is quite traditional by itself and places Christ alongside many other "next-generation" deities. Rather, it is the way in which this message is delivered that looks special, perhaps even unprecedented. Being born out of an attempt to reconcile contemporaneity with an outdated written tradition, it developed a special conversion technique which was later employed against competing religions. This technique consists in identifying the center point of a given tradition (its key "jot" or "tittle") and then using it as a universal term of reference, as something that could act as the "singularity" into which the whole of that tradition could collapse. This point is then aligned against its counterpart in the incoming tradition. This results in "shutting down" the control center of the outgoing tradition, destroying it theologically although not semiotically—preserving its symbolism intact and now able to use it selectively or reject it completely, depending on the spur of the moment.

Such a "conquest" is all the easier in those cases where the "opponent" religion has no established written tradition. The new religion in such circumstances can simply fill the vacancy and thus create a critical bridgehead from which it can pursue its advantage. Neither the pagan Europe, nor the twentieth-century Africa possessed any established written canon of their traditional religions and, unlike e.g., the religions of India, easily yielded to the advancement of Christianity. How exactly it happened and what are the prospects of African Traditional Religion in withstanding the onslaught of Abrahamic religions are the questions which we shall try to answer in the remaining chapters. But first, lest my readers think that I have forgotten the subject of this study, let us consider an African example of the above described process in some detail. For this purpose, I choose the story of Kwame Bediako (1945–2008), an eminent Ghanaian theologian and proponent of inculturation.

Case Study 5. The Conversion of Kwame Bediako

As we know from a recently published study,[2] Kwame Bediako's conversion was, strictly speaking, not from traditionalism but from atheism. However, as we also remember from the respective chapter of this book, atheism is virtually impossible in its pure form because it nearly always bears traces of the individual's previously rejected beliefs. The latter are often reinterpreted as metaphoric signs of his new convictions. The suppressed elements of traditional religion can thus easily recoil after conversion to Christianity. The "counterstrike" can be all the stronger the harder the original beliefs are suppressed. It may be also helpful to note that Kwame's father preserved his traditionalist beliefs almost to the end of life, converting only shortly before his death.

According to Bediako's own recollections, his true conversion to Christian faith (as opposed to his formal adoption of Christianity in his childhood) occurred in 1970[3] when he was pursuing his doctoral studies at the University of Bordeaux, France. His field of research was the oeuvre of U Tam'si, a francophone poet of Congolese extraction and a prominent

---

2. Sara J. Fretheim, *Kwame Bediako and African Christian Scholarship: Emerging Religious Discourse in Twentieth-Century Ghana* (African Christian Studies Series 13), Pickwick Publications, 2018.

3. Fretheim, *Kwame Bediako and African Christian Scholarship*, location 3374.

representative of the Negritude movement. Bediako's doctoral dissertation was nearly complete but made him feel unsatisfied because he was besieged by doubts whether something very important was still unsaid in his paper. Then the following chain of events ensued on the 10th of August:

> As he has recounted on numerous occasions, on that particular August day in Bordeaux he was *preparing to take a shower* when he noticed with shock that he was *crying*. With this realisation, he recounts, 'I just collapsed, fell to the floor *like a sack of potatoes*'; and, overcome with distress, wished for his life to be over. But in that moment something pivotal changed. As he describes it, 'suddenly I felt something new. I don't know where it came from, but it was a conviction that Jesus Christ was the *source* of life and the *key* to understanding . . .'[4]

What we have in this case is an archetypal description of "being born again" experience where the subject dies to his sinful past and rises to the new life in Christ. A closer look into the quoted passage will reveal that this experience follows a clearly defined semiotic pattern, very similar to the one presented in Paul's Areopagus speech.

Bediako's conversion starts with thinking about taking a shower. This detail may seem unimportant but why then did the convert keep mentioning it "on numerous occasions" as something without which the story would not be complete? Let us consider carefully the main meanings that "shower" has in English. Essentially, it can express two very different things: 1) "shower" as a synonym for "rain," i.e. a natural phenomenon and 2) "shower" in the sense of "bath in which water is poured from above," i.e. a manmade device. "Shower" as rain is a common symbol (and actual bringer) of fertility and, by extension, that of divine grace being poured down from heaven onto earth.

When Bediako thinks about taking a shower, he has only the second sense of the word in the "bright field" of his mind, yet he is also, most certainly, subconsciously aware of the first (primary) sense of it which he perceives as something tragically absent from his life. This double meaning of "shower" becomes Bediako's crucial *reference point* which allows him to establish a link between the incompleteness of the manmade world and the fulness of divine being; to build a bridge between an unreliable source of water provided by the secular civilization and the "well of water springing up into everlasting life" (John 4:14). The fact that such a connection has now been established is signified by his "crying," i.e. shedding tears both in alleviation of his "distress" and in evidence of the fact that the previously

---

4. Fretheim, *Kwame Bediako and African Christian Scholarship*, location 3384, emphasis added.

blocked flow of divine grace is now cleared of obstacles. Hitting on the newly discovered reference point gives to the convert access to the source of divine grace and puts him in possession of the key to its interpretation, i.e. opens the floodgates both of his mystical and intellectual cognition.

We should also bear in mind that Bediako, as a student of French, was at that time also aware of the very different sense distribution of the corresponding word for "shower" in the language he studied. The French for "shower" is "*douche*" and its etymology derives from the Italian cognate which originally meant "conduit." Such an origin straightaway positions "*douche*" as a "device" and not as a natural phenomenon, thus rendering problematic any associations with agricultural cults or divine grace. On the other hand, "conduit", by deriving from the Latin "*ducere*" (to lead), suggests the idea of a way out. But which way is that? It seems thus that for Bediako any attempts to think about his upcoming shower-taking in his "target language" would only exacerbate the same sensation of confusion described in the previous paragraph.

Next, Bediako's symbolic death is compared to "a sack of potatoes" heavily slumping onto the floor. As we can see, he uses quite a traditional metaphor which resonates with the already quoted verse from 1 Corinthians (15:36) where death is presented as a prerequisite to new life. It is also worth noting that, unlike Paul who does not specify the crop to be sown, Bediako identifies is as "potatoes." Although not an indigenous African crop, potatoes can pose as a substitute for yam—one of the staples of West African cuisine. Even though potatoes are not indigenous to Europe either, they have formed strong associations with that continent over the last three centuries. We can thus say that Bediako's leap into faith is not really from atheism but from the cult of Asase Ya—the goddess of earth known by many other names over West Africa—whose cult is steadily associated with yams offered to her. In the European setting, it is quite appropriate to substitute potatoes for yams. Thus, the fall of the sack of potatoes onto the floor can be, with a sufficient degree of certainty, considered to typify the fall of Asase Ya in the face of the rising figure of Jesus Christ.

It remains to be added that the resultant conversion prompted Bediako to rethink and rewrite his dissertation on U Tam'si "through the *eyes* of Christian faith." The previously missing component in Kwame's Weltanschauung finally clicked into place. In conclusion, we can say that the story of Bediako's conversion closely follows the general paradigm described in this chapter, where a superseding religious tradition asserts itself by collapsing into a single-point symbol which replaces its counterpart in the receding religious tradition. What holds good for Paul of Tarsus still holds for a twentieth-century West African theologian.

Chapter XIV

The Conquest: Joshua vs Josiah

UNLIKE TRADITIONAL RELIGIONS WHICH are mostly based on animistic experiences of the divine (or at least their present recollections), new-generation religions (Christianity included), as we saw in the previous chapter, appeal largely to faith. Consequently, the more people share that faith, the more convincing it should look. This is why expansion and proselytism play such an important role in Christian religion which is literally "programmed" to target other cultures by identifying their key reference points and replacing them with its own ones. Hence its famous missionary charge. However, this "conquest" does not always imply that the targeted culture is automatically earmarked for total annihilation and complete replacement by Christianity. As we also remember from the previous chapter, whenever a new religion comes across an array of symbols inherited from a substrate culture, it starts with disabling their key control centers, which allows it to invalidate those symbols, only to become able to recycle them for its own use. Yet this recycling remains a very selective process, as Christianity feels free to choose what to preserve and what to reject, often on very arbitrary and unclearly defined grounds.

The Christian conquest, as witnessed by mankind over the last couple of millennia, is not a completely unprecedented phenomenon—although certainly unprecedented by its global scale. As such, it had an important precedent—whether a historical or purely literary one, does not matter in our case—the conquest of Canaan by the Jews as described in the Book of Joshua. How true is that book in its representation of real events is not our concern here. It was the *contents* of that book that set a long-lasting pattern which determined the way in which pagan religions have been treated by Judaism and later by Christianity.

Contrary to the opinion of some secularists (Richard Dawkins among them), I do not find the Book of Joshua to be nothing but an outright glorification of genocide. Joshua's brutality in conquering other cultures may be too much for modern sensitivities but in historical perspective it is obvious that he simply followed the standard practice of his day. In those days (and we talk about the time frame that roughly falls on the thirteenth century BC) human beings still largely followed the prompts of their selfish genes that demanded complete destruction of an alien genetic pool. They were still unaware of or unheedful towards the rational laws of demographics that would argue for at least partial preservation of the conquered nation, both for the sake of enriching one's own genotype and assuring the minimum population density required for efficient economic management of the acquired territory. Viewed from that perspective, Joshua simply was doing the right thing when he ordered a mass slaughter of all tribes that the Israelites would overcome in their struggle for genetic survival. If the outcome of that struggle had turned out to be not in their favor (at least on one occasion) they would have expected exactly the same treatment in the hands of their enemies.

Yet the story of Joshua has also one remarkable feature which may allow us to assume that he actually opted for the most "humane" solution within his limited room for maneuver. Unable to oppose the diktat of his genes, he nonetheless shows some condescension towards the cultural memes[1] of the conquered people. This is what happens when the battle of Jericho is unconditionally decided in the Israelites' favor. The city, with all the inhabitants and properties it contains is definitely bound for destruction:

> And ye, in any wise keep yourselves from the accursed thing, lest ye make yourselves accursed, when ye take of the accursed thing, and make the camp of Israel a curse, and trouble it. But all the silver, and gold, and vessels of brass and iron, are consecrated unto the Lord: they shall come into the treasury of the Lord. [. . .] And they burnt the city with fire, and all that was therein: only the silver, and the gold, and the vessels of brass and of iron, they put into the treasury of the house of the Lord. (Josh 6:18–19, 24)

---

1. It is beyond my grasp why Richard Dawkins fails to spot this remarkable fact when he quotes the same passage from Joshua in *The God Delusion*. Instead, he engages in a sentimental talk on modern Israeli schoolchildren being confused about the moral of this story (p. 289 ff). When was the last time he reread *The Selfish Gene*?

Why did Joshua decide to spare nothing except the metal vessels captured during the conquest of Jericho? Certainly not because they were intended to be used later for storage or cooking in the conquerors' daily life. And, even more certainly, not because the Israelites considered them to be things of any artistic value. To suggest that would mean to slip into flagrant anachronism and attribute secular ideas to people whose consciousness was uniformly religious. Rather, the vessels are "consecrated unto the Lord" as an act of cultural assimilation. Having been appropriated as trophies they are treated as symbols that have lost the link between their signifier and signified. They have become artefacts whose original meaning is abolished and which can now be safely reassigned to a new cultural signified. They are used to enrich the collection of symbolic forms for the winner culture. To use another anachronistic expression (this time a deliberate one) we can say that this passage from Joshua describes one of the first examples of *inculturation* in human history.

I feel tempted to speculate what a modern Joshua would look like. Perhaps nowadays he would be a liberal Catholic missionary who would be doing his best to preserve the ancient lore and artefacts of traditional culture, while insisting at the same time that their preservation is conditional on their being recycled as subordinate symbols of the true religion. However, I will not pursue the subject because I have promised to engage only in observations, not in modelling. Still, I believe that Joshua should be given credit for the little step he took in planting what, in my opinion, was the germ of man's changing attitudes towards things that originally do not belong to his tribe.

Another thing about this story that is truly remarkable is the consensus of modern biblical scholars that the Book of Joshua was written in the time of King Josiah who reigned between 640 and 609 BC and who was famous for his vigorous campaign to eradicate all cults that suggested the worship of any deities other than YHWH. His first action under that campaign targeted exactly what Joshua thought fit to preserve:

> And the king commanded Hilkiah the high priest, and the priests of the second order, and the keepers of the door, to bring forth out of the temple of the Lord all the vessels that were made for Baal, and for the grove, and for all the host of heaven: and he burned them without Jerusalem in the fields of Kidron, and carried the ashes of them unto Bethel. (2 Kgs 23:4)

This is followed, of course, by the destruction of everything and anyone else associated with the idolatrous cult, including the slaughter of its ministers (23:5–20). These further actions certainly look logical in the light of the king's relentless policy towards the affirmation of consistent monotheism. What does not, however, look logical to me is that Josiah seems to act in a manner contrary to that of Joshua as far as the sacred vessels are concerned. If the Book of Joshua was indeed written, or at least sketched, during Josiah's reign, its protagonist would probably feature as a perfect example of what had been done on a similar occasion many centuries before. Why then does Josiah not follow that example? Why does he not order to rededicate the vessels pillaged from the temple of Baal to their new owner, even though he "appropriately" chooses to destroy everything else? It may be either because the actual Book of Joshua had not yet been written or looked different from the way we know it. But whatever the reasons (if there were any) one thing can be stated with certainty: Josiah is a very different type of religious activist; he indiscriminately targets alien memes with no attempt at inculturation. From modern perspective, he is an example of cultural retrogression, someone who prefers destruction to recreation.

The similarity of names of these two characters may come in handy in presenting the two opposite approaches to cultural conquest: Joshua and Josiah—the one who cares (if only to a very limited extent) for alien cultural heritage and the one who does not. Conventionally, their names can be used to denote two different ways which the winner religion can pursue with respect to the one it intends to replace. The way of Joshua and the way of Josiah are equally traceable in the history of Christianity encountering primal religions.

If we now turn again to the Apostle Paul and try see the predominant attitude of his writings, we can see that in most cases he follows Joshua when it comes to determining the fate of symbols which at first sight seem to clash with his own doctrine. His usual solution in such cases is to declare that a given symbol has forfeited its sacred properties and thus become a nonentity or, in Paul's own words "sounding brass or a clanging cymbal" (1 Cor 13:1), i.e. signifier without signified.

Let us take one example from his famous Epistle to the Galatians which contains Paul's discourse on circumcision (5:2–12). It is well-known that in the Jewish law circumcision is viewed as a sign of man's union with God—for obvious reason: cutting off one's foreskin symbolically represents removal of the cover that creates an obstacle to communication, with the penis interpreted as an organ of that communication, which, being circumcised, becomes exposed to outside energies. Yet we remember that, according to Paul, the whole Law loses its validity once the believer has accepted Christ as his savior. As soon as this act of faith is committed, whatever used to have sacred significance now loses it without acquiring anything in replacement. What used to be an important rite of initiation, becomes a meaningless surgical procedure. Paul argues that an attempt to restore the original signification of that rite would automatically reinstitute the previous validity of the Law in its entirety. Circumcision in this interpretation becomes a randomly chosen reference point (as any other Jewish rite could act in that capacity) through which (as we have already seen a few times before) the new religion is able to disqualify the old one.

Paul does not stop here. Not only does he nullify the sacred symbolism of circumcision—he also switches from naught to negative by assigning it a pejorative connotation. In order to do so, he shunts the associative link from the idea of "opening" to that of "cutting off" (5:12). Persevering, he says, in the opinion that circumcision is still necessary for union with God actually results in cutting oneself off from God or in emasculating oneself (the verse can be understood either way). Both circumcision as a symbol and circumcision as a surgical procedure have lost their sacred meanings and now have come to express self-mutilation both in the physical and spiritual sense. I find this passage in Galatians a very bold piece of liberal theology and an elegant exercise in semiotics of religion.

So much for the Jewish symbolism. What about the pagan one? Let us take another famous example from the First Epistle to the Corinthians. In chapter 8, Paul discusses whether it is appropriate for a Christian to eat "food sacrificed to idols." He thinks that to do so does not mean to commit idolatry. As long as the idol is stripped clear of all its symbolic connotations ("we know that an idol is nothing in the world"—8:4) even sitting "at meat in the idol's temple" (8:10) will constitute nothing but an ordinary act of eating—something perfectly neutral in terms of religious affiliation: "But meat commendeth us not to God: for neither, if we eat, are we the better; neither, if we eat not, are we the worse" (8:8).

It is only when this deliberate parading of one's immunity to neutralized symbols can be misconstrued by less advanced Christians for whom idols may still retain some residual spirituality that Paul advises to refrain from doing it publicly, not to jeopardize "the conscience of him which is weak" (8:10). Viewed in this light, his later call to "flee from idolatry" (10:14) assumes a purely ethical, rather than theological meaning in the sense of "not to let your semiotically less expert neighbor become victim of his ignorance." It is with this sense in mind that the following passage should be read:

> What say I then? that the idol is any thing, or that which is offered in sacrifice to idols is any thing? But I say, that the things

which the Gentiles sacrifice, they sacrifice to devils, and not to God: and I would not that ye should have fellowship with devils. Ye cannot drink the cup of the Lord, and the cup of devils: ye cannot be partakers of the Lord's table, and of the table of devils. Do we provoke the Lord to jealousy? are we stronger than he? (10:19–22)

As long as the idol is not "any thing" for us, we are safe to behave in any manner, including those extreme cases when some of our acts can bear formal resemblance to pagan "fellowship with devils." It is only when doing so we start, at least partially, to *mean it*, i.e. to revive the previously severed links that refer the idol to its spiritual signified, that we can "provoke the Lord to jealousy"—a feeling completely justified on God's part, considering that we would thus deny him the spiritual monopoly that we believe him to possess. This is another bold incursion into the field of liberal semiotics.

One again, I feel tempted to ask a question similar to the one that bothered me with regard to Joshua: What would Paul be like—not even in our days, but in the days when Christianity for the first time became the official religion of the Empire? Would he still allow his followers to come and "sit at meat in the idol's temple" whenever they felt like doing so (e.g., because they had nowhere else to eat) as long as they were not feeling tempted to switch their spiritual allegiances? Would he still leave the pagan temples and their idols in their places as mere "nothings" or perhaps as artefacts of some aesthetic value? (In the case of Paul that would not sound so anachronistic as in the case of Joshua.) Or would he rather have those temples closed and statues pulled down in order to avoid possible temptation for those who do not feel themselves to be completely free from superstition? One thing is clear: for Paul it is not essential whether a certain thing may have undesirable symbolic connotations, as the latter can be always declared null and void by a single act of faith, i.e. moving into a different coordinate system where old references are no longer valid. Adopting such a system to a full extent allows Paul (and potentially anyone else) to become "all things to all men" as he proudly declares in the same epistle between the two previously quoted passages (9:22).

We are now going finally to take leave of past centuries and concentrate entirely on contemporary Africa in the rest of this book. This means that we, at last, can fully dedicate ourselves to the main subject—the relationship between African Traditional Religion and Christianity in the early twenty-first century. Everything I have said before can therefore be considered as a long prolegomenon to the discussion which intends to address some current controversies that exist on the issue. I do apologize to those of my readers who feel that I should have come "straight to the point" much earlier but I also think that what has been said so far will contribute to a better understanding of what I am going to say in the last three chapters.

Specifically, I want to pursue the path outlined in this chapter where we have tried to differentiate between two possible attitudes to a heterogenous tradition encountered by an expanding religion: that of Josiah and that of Joshua. If we wanted to translate them into modern idiom, the closest equivalents we could find would be probably "exclusivism" and "inclusivism." The advantage of these, more common, terms is that they are self-explanatory. An exclusivist is obviously someone who excludes his religion from all others whose existence he finds to be unnecessary or perhaps even dangerous. Such a person would treat with indifference anything that does not belong to his religion. And if he found that anything outside his religion poses an obstacle to the latter's development, he would do his best to get rid of the former, even if that meant destroying it completely. His behavior would thus more resemble that of Josiah during his religious reform.

Conversely, an inclusivist, as the name also shows, while coming across anything different from his own religion, would at least theoretically assume that the alien tradition may contain something that can better express the ideas on which his religion is based. Although such a person still believes that his religion is superior to others which it must supplant, he would not exclude borrowing at least some symbolic forms that can be assimilated and put to use within his own system. This is what Joshua did when he ordered to collect the gold and silver vessels captured at Jericho and to rededicate them to the God of the Israelites.

However, there is sometimes no strict border between exclusivism and inclusivism, as we saw in the example of the Apostle Paul who can be indifferent but not necessarily intolerant to non-Christian symbols. At most, he thinks they pose only an indirect threat to his religion—to those of its converts who are not yet strong enough in their faith. Potentially at least, that may mean that at some further stage of its development, Christianity may adopt certain symbols it initially considered incompatible or harmful, provided that they are first neutralized and then assigned new meanings within the Christian system. The main problem about Paul is, therefore, that both exclusivists and inclusivists can appeal to his teachings, depending on their *ad hoc* interpretations of controversial points.

There is also a third option, a fairly recent one, that was certainly unknown either in the time of Joshua or that of Josiah. It is called *pluralism*. Unlike the previous two choices, pluralism resigns any claims to assimilation of other traditions and declares their equal value with its own tradition. Essentially, it means finally discarding the idea of conquest and supplanting it with that of tolerance and mutual respect. In the extreme-case scenario, it means that each party to the argument possesses the truth only partially and will only gain from their dialogue and rapprochement. Usually, pluralism avoids answering the question how two given parties can be equally right if they proceed on diametrically opposite assumptions. Pluralism, therefore, has its own problems and cannot be always recommended as a universal solution, even in secularist circles.

In the remaining part of the book we shall examine the semiotic aspects of these three approaches, trying to find out what they imply for the future relationship between African Traditional Religion and Christianity.

Chapter XV

Exclusivism

MOST OF THE MISSIONARY effort undertaken during the twentieth-century Christian "conquest" was essentially exclusivist in its nature. Josiah usually dominated over Joshua, or, more specifically, any manifestations of Joshuanism (aimed mostly at preservation of material artefacts, often taken out of their religious context) usually originated from secular powers (colonial administrations and scholarly community) rather than ecclesiastical ones.

Whenever the church came across a religious concept for which a Christian parallel could be traced, the former would be usually declared inferior to its Christian counterpart and therefore not worth preservation. Thus, the Supreme Being of many African religions was normally considered inferior to the Christian God, because the former would be found too transcendental and uninvolved in man's everyday life or metaphysical salvation. Very often, things that looked different from the Christian doctrine, would be declared diabolical and bound for eradication. This rule applied both to ideas (e.g., polytheistic deities), rituals (e.g., ancestor cults) and certainly to nearly all artefacts (e.g., fetishes and shrines).

In the second half of the twentieth century and especially after the Second Vatican Council, this missionary zeal started to cool down, gradually giving way to the policy of inculturation. How/whether that policy has been successful is the question we shall try to answer in the next chapter. However, exclusivism is far from being dead in Africa. On the contrary, it has been steadily increasing in the last couple of decades. Josiah's mantle has been picked up by the numerous Pentecostal (charismatic/spiritual) movements which at the moment are acting as the main destructive force directed against all forms of African indigenous culture. This may certainly look strange to many outside observers not immediately familiar with Africa's contemporary situation. Indeed, one can easily understand why missionaries from Europe encouraged local population to burn their fetishes, drain their sacred ponds or cut down their sacred groves; but why should Africans themselves apply such destructive policies to their own heritage?

The answer, I suppose, can be found in the semiotic properties of destruction. Destruction often acts as a symbol of renewal; to destroy often means to purify everything around, to erase the errors of the past and recollections of one's sinful deeds; to rend the veil between man and God; to wipe the slate clean and start from scratch. Such desires are deeply ingrained in human psyche in general but are especially pronounced among the cultures of the Northern Hemisphere (cf. e.g., potlatch among the natives of North America where mass destruction of artefacts is an occasion for celebration). Even Jesus himself, with all his avowed conservatism, could display very similar trends in his teaching when he would something like this: "I am come to send fire on the earth and what will I, if it be already kindled?" (Luke 12:49). Africa, especially the Sahel part of it, has its own visual type of mass extermination– when dead vegetation catches fire over vast expanses of space at the peak of the dry season (a spectacle I have witnesses myself). When a casual traveler finds himself in the midst of that "world conflagration," he may understand why so many Africans take destruction as a regular (seasonal) affair. He may also suspect that modern African Pentecostalism can be an indigenous phenomenon, much as it may be thought to have been imported from North America.

There is a downside to this *auto-da-fé*: It creates a dangerous shortage of expressive means. Making God a blank, destitute of any symbols, can, as we have seen in our discussion of monotheism, trigger the process of His disappearance, i.e. sliding first into wordless mysticism and potentially even into outspoken atheism. Fundamentalist Christianity solves this problem by exploiting negative symbols—the remnants of conquered cultures which now stand for everything that opposes the true God and bound to be eliminated. This process of elimination has to be carried on indefinitely because it is the only way at the fundamentalist's disposal to maintain God's signification—to keep showing *what God is not like*; to fuel the ecstatic perception of God by burning His false representations. As the process has to be constantly maintained, it always stays in need of "fuel"—every act of God's affirmation demands a certain amount of fetishes to be burnt and a certain number of evil spirits to be cast out.

Obviously, no truly indigenous culture can keep up with that demand for "consumables." However, they do not really have to be truly indigenous. Anything that can stand for devil's opposition to God and has some African connotation can be produced *en masse* and later used to ensure a sufficient supply of symbol to be destroyed. A good example in that respect is cowry shells. They are ubiquitous in Africa. They were once used as money and can, should need be, serve as representation of an African "Mammon" who, according to the Gospel (Matt 6:24; Luke 16:13) cannot be worshiped at the same time with God. But because cowry shells can be assigned such a connotation, it is believed that can just as easily be appropriated by African indigenous deities, who are supposed to be no less evil and mercantile than their Middle Eastern prototype. Thus cowry shells can be considered capable of housing local African deities[1] who are now downgraded to the status of lower spirits hostile to the Christian God. Therefore, cowry shells should be discouraged from being worn as a decoration or, even more so, from being used for divination or in any other communicative context. They are bound for continuous destruction as a sign of the Christian's permanent struggle against the forces of evil—therefore their stock should be maintained at due level at all times.

We know from the Gospel that we should not get too carried away fighting evil spirits because we risk making things worse:

> When the unclean spirit is gone out of a man, he walketh through dry places, seeking rest; and finding none, he saith, I will return unto my house whence I came out. And when he cometh, he findeth it swept and garnished. Then goeth he, and taketh to him seven other spirits more wicked than himself; and they enter in, and dwell there: and the last state of that man is worse than the first. (Matt 12:43–45; Luke 11:24–26)

For Pentecostal Christians, however, worse is better—the more enemies around, the more opportunity to show off one's zeal in combatting them and, eventually, the higher chance of salvation.

Some Pentecostalists apparently go as far as to borrow not only negative but also positive powers from traditional religion, which they then "recode" as Christian virtues. Such acts, if they are true, can be considered as nascent elements of Joshuanism. Thus, if we are to believe the Internet, there is evidence that some Christian ministers in Africa borrow (buy?) their healing capabilities from traditional practitioners in order to perform some spectacular feats in public. Yet some of them are allegedly just as ungrateful

---

1. The source of that information is personal conversation with my Ghanaian friend, Comfort Appiah, which I duly acknowledge here.

as they are arrogant, because they express contempt for their miracle suppliers as people who do not know the true God. Such behavior is, however, generally condemned.[2]

Although extensively appealing to Christian tradition (Jesus as a worker of miracles) Pentecostalism significantly departs from tradition in its overreliance on thaumaturgy (miracle-working) as its preferred means of signification. Paradoxically as it may sound, the modern man is better susceptible to the idea of the miraculous than even a century ago. This is because modern technology is becoming increasingly sophisticated and no longer understandable to non-specialists. There is no essential semiotic difference between turning the switch to light a room and laying hands on a parishioner possessed with an evil spirit. In both cases we see no connection between the action and its effect. In both cases we do not know "how exactly it happens." But perhaps the technical device looks even less understandable and therefore more miraculous. We can still see why touching a someone's body can effect a cure, but why changing the position of a switch causes the light to turn on, most of us are unable to tell. If we still persist and try to find out "what is inside," we shall not be any more enlightened: all we shall be able to see is some sort of "fetish"—a certain combination of various lines and shapes whose interaction we cannot understand.

But perhaps even a specialist will find it hard to explain (even to himself) how something that originally exists as a drawing (a two-dimensional fetish?) can be later embodied as a piece of hardware with some practical application. The transition from the ideal to the material is beyond our grasp too. We are increasingly surrounded by all sorts of miracles in our daily life. From that point of view, Pentecostal emphasis on thaumaturgy is merely a reflection of that trend in Christian liturgy.

But it is not only Pentecostal zeal that contributes to the triumphant progress of Christianity across Africa and to the abandonment of indigenous religions. Other semiotic concerns must be taken into account too.

The fact that Christianity is an imported religion, plays, for example, much to its advantage. We have already discussed in Case Study 1 how Jesus' complexion positions him against indigenous gods as someone who promises of more thorough experience of renewal. Can we then assume that the best gods are often foreign ones? It is quite instructive in that connection to

---

2. Top Pastors Render Apology To Akonodi Shrine http://m.peacefmonline.com/pages/local/social/201403/192280.php, last visited on 06/12/2019

see, for example, the role played by Egypt in the religions of Africa and those of the Middle East.

It is a common notion among many African intellectuals that their traditional religion has roots stretching back to Ancient Egypt. Some of them—like Sheikh Anta Diop—have even tried to prove that the ancient Egyptians belonged predominantly to the black race. Equally, for the founders of Judaism—the authors of the Pentateuch—it was just as important to repeatedly stress that their religion began with their God leading His chosen people out of Egypt. However, it is just as likely that the opposite is true: that the Egyptian culture was not the source but the product of two major cultural streams that met—or better to say, collided—on the flood plains of the Nile, taking their humble origins in sub-Saharan Africa and on the mountains of Transjordan. Such a collision could have resulted in an unprecedented surge of cultural achievement to be unsurpassed by its "mother cultures" for many centuries to follow. To borrow a metaphor from geophysics, we can say that an encounter of that scale could have caused the rise of the pyramids in the same way that the collision between a split-off part of Gondwana and the mainland of Laurasia caused the rise of the Himalayas on the border of the Indian subcontinent.

Both ancient Israelites and modern Africans were later fascinated by the enormous cultural stature of Egypt and neither of them recognized their own reflection in that mirror. This is not surprising as the Egyptian culture by the time it shined back on its "underdeveloped" progenitors, had thoroughly digested its heritage and came up with something that outwardly resembled none of them. Both Africans and Jews found it equally important to insist on their own culture being imported from a far-away land—although it was done in different contexts: that of denial in the case of Jews and that of appropriation in the case of Africans.

When the nineteenth-century missionaries from Europe finally made it to sub-Saharan Africa, its many recipients also regarded it as something that had come from afar—from a strange land of white creatures—all the more appropriate to substitute for their native culture. The fact that Jesus himself is reported to have spent a considerable part of his life in Egypt has to some extent contributed to that perception.

It is often hard for an indigenous culture to resist the sweeping force of Christianity—a religion which, as we have seen in previous chapters, is specially designed to target the center-points of the culture it intends to displace. Worse still for the indigenous religion, the more organized it is, the more established are the traditions it is based upon, the more easily it may fall prey to Christianity, as the easier it will be for the latter to identify its targets. From that perspective, those African nations which by the time of Christianity's arrival had developed a strong statehood with well-defined political and religious institutions became more vulnerable to the foreign intruder than those whose political and religion organization was less articulated. A comparison between two neighboring West African peoples—Ashanti and Ewe—will yield a good example.

The Ashanti people, at the time of arrival of European missionaries, were famous for their sharply outlined political and religious hierarchy: everyone—from the king at the top down to his lowest subject at the bottom—had a clearly prescribed set of functions and duties. The structure was rigid and capable only of limited adjustment. It left very little room for maneuver, very little chance for opposing equally convincing means of expression to the ones imposed to intruders. The rigidity of the Ashanti religious tradition made it especially susceptible to missionary efforts to dismantle it. It had almost no defensive weapons at its disposal, because it had never tried to argumentatively prove its rightness in the first place. As a result, most of the Ashanti people are at present professed Christians.

The state of Ewe society presents a very different picture and so does their religion. The Ewe have never developed a full-fledged political structure. They have no nation state but exist in a permanent cross-border fluidity, when many of them regularly migrate between Ghana and Togo. Their religion, commonly known as Voodoo (Vodun, Vodon, Vodoun, Vodou) shows the same flexibility. To an outside observer it seems to be in a constant state of rethinking, reinventing, and redevelopment. Every major celebration and even every next throw of figures by an Afa diviner causes a reshuffle in the game. The outcome of such events is unpredictable—it cannot be known in advance which specific deities, ancestors or simply "guest spirits" will appear and which participants of the festival they will possess. The system gets deconstructed and reconstructed every time it is put in operation. Between the two poles there is a moment of suspense, when primeval chaos sets in for a short while.

Such a religion proves to be more resistant to missionary intrusion. This is because the missionary (who is nowadays likelier to be a Pentecostal preacher) never knows where to deal the next strike—his opponent resembles the mythical Proteus who would change appearances every time the attacker tried to seize him. Indeed, Voodoo remains one of the few indigenous traditions in West Africa that enjoy relative wellbeing. Although it is not the religion of the majority anymore, at least it is professed by a significant minority.

On the whole, the exclusivist (Josiahan) type of Christianity, despite being the anthropologist's nightmare, looks like a convincing and healthy solution for today's Africa—judging by the rate at which it has been acquiring new followers in recent times. Its main advantages are simplicity and universal applicability. It is the most cosmopolitan of all forms of Christianity. Adhering to that movement makes many Africans feel part of a worldwide movement that is capable of bringing their continent up to international standards.

The downside of that project is, of course, the danger for Africa to lose its uniqueness and individuality. But this is the downside of all globalization in general—a trend which envisages a world where everyone would wear the same clothes, watch the same TV programs and say the same prayers, asking the Almighty to make him look just like everyone else. Whether Africa really wants (or deserves) such a solution, is for the Africans themselves to decide. But before any decision can be made, it is worth knowing whether there are any viable alternatives to the above solution. It is these alternatives that we are going to consider in the last two chapters.

Chapter XVI

Inclusivism

As we noted in chapter XIV, inclusivism generally assumes that, although the indigenous tradition must give way to the newcomer, some of its elements, usually referred to as "values," may be deemed appropriate for preservation. In semiotic idiom that means that certain religious symbols (and sometimes even doctrines) can be considered to be better (or at least not inferior) expressions of similar ideas contained in the new religion, or in some cases to be dealing with notions missing from the new religion. We also provided the archetypal example of Joshua who chose to save the vessels captured at the taking of Jericho. These vessels were re-sanctified for ceremonial use in the cult of YHWH, rather than destroyed like everything else seized in that battle.

We also said that the main modern proponent of this line of action is the Roman Catholic Church which, having the transactions of Vatican II as its guidance, has been officially pursuing the policy of inculturation which purports to selectively preserve certain cultural values of indigenous peoples as long as they are deemed not to contradict the main tenets of Christianity. As such, the Catholic Church looks well-qualified for this task, as it has centuries-long experience of assimilating religious symbols which initially did not belong to it. Thus, the custom of making pancakes on Shrove Tuesday or painting eggs at Easter were originally attributes of predecessor fertility cults, which the church found possible to appropriate, reinterpreting them as Christian (or at least religiously neutral) symbols.

However, if we ask ourselves how successful inculturation has been in Africa over the last fifty years, the likeliest answer will be: only to a very limited extent. The church's firm presence on that continent and its close contacts with local population have not resulted in any significant changes of its rites and absolutely no changes in any of its doctrines, even minor ones.

Everyone who has at least once attended a Catholic mass in Africa will be able to tell how un-African it feels. The only difference between what one can see in Europe and what one can observe in Africa is that drumming and dancing, rather than Gregorian chant and organ-playing, may now accompany the Great Entrance, the Offertory, the Consecration or the period after the Holy Communion. Also, African rhythms can be occasionally discerned in the chants sung by the congregation, although most of them are still perfectly European. In all other respects, if the observer ignores the motley attires of the parishioners (and sometimes the traditional African elements in the priest's vesture) he can be confused with regard to his geographical location.

One cannot say that absolutely no attempts have been made towards making the Catholic service look more African. Yet such attempts almost invariably run into a brick wall. Here is, for example, the testimony of the Ghanaian Archbishop Peter K. Sarpong (b. 1933), a very respected authority on interfaith dialogue:

> In my research, I came to the conclusion that the externals of the Mass are not attractive to the faithful. At Mass, there appears to be a one-man show. There is no personal touch; there is no spontaneity; there is no celebration; there is no flexibility; there is no real participation. […]
>
> It was with these in mind that in the 1970s I wrote my own Mass. I took into account the key characteristics of Asante sacrifice, namely, full participation, flexibility, joy, celebration, relevance and adaptability. […] I submitted it to my priests to criticise. The reaction ranged from downright condemnation to half-hearted commendation. […] Some priests from Ireland even insulted me that I was comparing the unique sacrifice of the Holy Mass to pagan practices!! […]
>
> So, I recoiled into my shell.[1]

Two things, I believe, should be noted in the quoted extract: 1) the general fear of borrowing and 2) the fear of borrowing certain things that are perceived as incompatible with Christian religion.

---

1. Sarpong, *Peoples Differ*, 114–115.

The first kind of fear reflects the ancient notion of unity (identity) between form and contents, signifier and signified, as discussed in our introductory chapters. The prevailing belief in this case is that by changing the form (or introducing a new form) we can also change the contents, i.e. not only disturb the ritualistic structure of a given religion but also affect its dogmatic and doctrinal basis. Even minor changes can be fatal, for, as we read in Galatians, "A little leaven leaveneth the whole lump" (5:9). From this point of view any proposed borrowing into the Roman Mass should be considered heretical and therefore rejected. Should it happen otherwise, there is a fear that the Catholic Church will lose its global uniformity or, worse, that its African branches will engage in increasingly syncretic cults—similar to many African Instituted Churches (AIC) whose belonging to Christianity has been often disputed. However, such an approach seems to clash with the slogans of Vatican II and cannot be used as practical guidance. This is probably why, according to Archbishop Sarpong, those who at first detracted his initiative later wrote to him "to apologise . . . for their insults."[2]

On a more subtle level, some proposed borrowings may seem to contradict not the letter but the spirit of Christianity. Thus, in the passage quoted above, "joy" and "celebration" are listed among the key notions that have prompted Sarpong's search for liturgical reform. On the surface level, there may seem to be nothing wrong with them: the Mass *is* a celebration as it marks the renewal of God's covenant with man every time it is pontificated. Yet this celebration of a very special nature: it equally highlights God's *absence* as it does his *presence*. The hero of the occasion, the heavenly Bridegroom, is not with his earthly Bride—he has promised to come back in an uncertain future. Until his return happens, there is no cause for full-scale festivities—it is more about patiently waiting in anticipation of the glory to come. All celebration has, therefore, to be low-profile, all expressions of joy muted, all lighting subdued, all music in minor key. Even the magnificent sizes of many church buildings can contribute to the sensation of empty space, a void that can be filled only on the arrival of their true Owner (see also our Case Study 2).

From this point of view, even such seemingly innocent things as drumming and dancing may look out of place on this occasion. Drumming and dancing would look more appropriate to greet the Bridegroom's arrival, not his departure. And although his presence may be symbolically or (as in the case of the Catholic Church) even physically recreated during the Mass, it happens only for a very short time, as his recreated body is almost immediately consumed by the pious congregation.

2. Sarpong, *Peoples Differ*, p. 115.

Let us take another ritual which is commonly promoted as a symbol of rapprochement between the African and Christian traditions—libation. Its major revival in West Africa is credited to Kwame Nkrumah in the late 1950s. Since then, it has been gaining an increasing number of champions among the Christians (with Archbishop Sarpong as one of its vigorous proponents). Yet, if we view libation as a semiotic action, we shall quickly discover that in its outward appearance it looks contrary to what happens during the Christian Mass where wine is *collected* into the chalice as a symbol (or physical recreation in the Catholic case) of the Savior's blood. To pour some of its contents onto the ground would mean to sacrifice something that has already been sacrificed, to have collected the precious blood of deity only to wastefully spill it. The problem of semiotic incompatibility between libation and eucharist can turn out to be sharper than it may seem at first sight.

Facing difficulties in engrafting some "cuttings" from African Traditional Religion to the Christian "stock," religious thinkers (both from the Christian and traditionalist camps) have been trying to take a step in the opposite direction—to use traditional religion as the "stock" and elements of Christianity (usually the figure of Christ himself) as the "cutting." Thus, over the last couple of decades, Jesus has been increasingly promoted in ecumenical literature as an African character, among whose many traditional attributes could be listed those of "the Greatest Ancestor," "the Master of Initiation," "the Head Healer," etc.

The problem with these designations is that they emphasize the divine nature of Jesus and tend to downplay his human side which is considered to be of equal importance in Christianity where he is not only the King of Kings but also the Man of Sorrows. We have seen that at least in some African traditions, there are personages who can be treated as potential Christ figures (see chapter XII). However, it would be much easier to apply the "Man of Sorrows" idea to a local character, rather than to someone who is solemnly brought from overseas as a world Savior to be embraced by the "groaning creation" of Africa. It would be contrary to African hospitality to denigrate a person like that.

Thus, when Kofi Bempah, whom we have already quoted in our chapter on monotheism, writing from the traditionalist's perspective, describes Jesus' ascent from humanity to divinity, he makes a praiseworthy effort to translate Christian notions into the idiom of Akan Traditional Religion. Yet one has to note that the movement described in Bempah's book is always one-directional, always upwards, without a hint of *kenosis* that orthodox Christian theology equally attributes to that person:

> Jesus [. . .] started his spiritual journey as a messenger of God.
> [. . .]
> Later, when Jesus Grew in Wisdom, He called Himself the Son of God. The authority of a prince is far higher than a mere courtier who runs an errand for the king. Thus Jesus assumed greater authority but still saw Himself as different from the Father. When He finally realised his unitive identity with God, He could proclaim, 'The Father and I are One'. He became a Nana.[3]

He may have become a nana, i.e. acquired the status equal to that of an Akan king. However, we cannot lose sight of the fact that, according to the Gospel, the highest status he achieved in his earthly life—arguably, during his Transfiguration—was witnessed only by three of his disciples (Mt 17:1, Mk 9:2, Lk 9:28) and in no way publicly proclaimed. It is true that the story of Transfiguration has many features of a *rite de passage*, being preceded by a six-day marginal period (eight according to Luke) and sanctified by the apparition of two illustrious ancestors—Moses and Elijah. However, it is just as true that this solemn enthronement was followed by Jesus' being sentenced to death by the Jewish highest authority, the Sanhedrin. In African terms that would obviously mean that his nana status was thus revoked.

The poetry of Afua Kuma, so often promoted as an example of perfect assimilation of Christian ideas by an indigenous African, displays, in fact, the same one-sidedness. Here we have Jesus as "the great Rock," "the Big Tree," "incomparable Diviner," "the Hunter gone to the deep forest" to allay people's fears of Sasabonsam[4] etc. The images are vivid and genuinely African, but it is always the Jesus who stands on the top of Mount Tabor, not the Jesus who hangs on the cross that dominates Kuma's passionate overflows. Does she express the authentically Christian view of the Savior or does she Africanize him too much?

Such a partial overlap between African Traditionalism and Christianity is even more visible when we descend from the top occupied by supreme beings to a lower tier of religion populated by subordinate spirits. It is often suggested, for example, that the numerous and ubiquitous ancestor cults in Africa find their parallel in the Catholic Communion of Saints. Yet all attempts to approximate these two categories of spiritual entities have resulted

---

3. Bempah, *Akan Traditional Religion*, 290–91.
4. Afua Kuma, *Jesus of the Deep Forest*, 5 and 20.

more in highlighting their differences than their similarities. The Christian saints are first and foremost those who have been successful in following the example of Christ. The surest way to be canonized is to suffer a violent death while professing one's faith in the face of those who negate it, i.e. to accept the crown of martyrdom. If the indifferent world denies you that crown, the second-best way might be to make yourself suffer self-inflicted deprivations, i.e. to restrict the amount of consumed food, to shorten the time of sleep, to engage in continuous prayer or to impose on oneself any other material inconveniences in an attempt to make one's life more spiritual (see also the "Plenitude and Deficiency" section in the next chapter). Only the least preferable option would be to lead a troublesome, although pious, life and to die "full of days" surrounded by your disciples or admirers.

If we now turn to African Traditional Religion, we shall see this hierarchy reversed. The most venerated are those who lived their lives to the full, who accumulated enough possessions to ensure comfortable existence for their offspring and whose death can be viewed as a logical completion of one's life achievements, first of all the material ones (welfare, high social ranking etc.). The higher those achievements, the more chance one has to carry on rendering services to one's family/community after death. Is it because these beliefs are still very much alive that the prosperity gospel ideology finds such a fertile field in modern Africa? It may be harder to answer that question than it may seem at first sight, considering that the teaching of prosperity gospel originated in North America, rather than Africa. But it is not a task of this book to offer a critique of that school anyway.

It is true that the above-outlined attitude is not all-prevailing. Indeed, it knows some remarkable exceptions: thus, at least in some African traditions, the ghosts of those who died a violent death are believed to acquire special supernatural powers unavailable to respected ancestors. Those powers may be later utilized by surviving members of the family/community. Yet the role of such characters is relatively minor and can neither replace the ancestors nor even compare with them in importance.

The common denominator to which researchers of religion usually try to bring the saints and ancestors is the fact that both are supposed to be *venerated*, rather than *worshiped*. Veneration in this context, due to its lesser importance, is believed to allow greater freedom of attitude and greater ease with which similarities, rather than differences could be emphasized. The main problem that arises at this juncture is that of distinction between worship and veneration. For example: Does offering prayers or sacrifices to a spiritual entity necessitate its designation as worship or can it be still, under certain circumstances, classified as veneration? But perhaps the solution in this case would be not to care too much about this distinction and to label any forms of cult offered to spiritual entities other than the Supreme Being as veneration without getting into unnecessary details. Such a solution would certainly endow Christianity with greater flexibility in assimilating (or perhaps simply coexisting with) those traditions with which it has no full correspondence.

Case Study 6. The Big House

I want now to give an illustration of that "flexibility" using an example from my native land—the Republic of Moldova (formerly part of the Soviet Union). I want to do so not because I am eager to put this tiny country on the map but because I find this example really illustrative and even striking. I apologize for breaking my promise not to go out of Africa in the final chapters of my book but I hope I will be excused because, for once on this occasion, I am going to speak entirely from my own experience. And because it is my experience, I have never cared to investigate how unique Moldova is in that respect. However, being no specialist in the Balkan culture to which Moldova at least marginally belongs I leave this question to experts in the field. All I want now is to give a vivid example of how far ancestor veneration may go in a predominantly (if not even exclusively) Christian community.

Anyone who has at least once spent a night in the Moldovan countryside will be able to confirm that every established household there nearly always has *two* houses within its compound: a small one and a large one. This may look nothing unusual at first sight but the striking thing about it is that it is the small house, not the large one, that is normally used for dwelling. Quite often the tiny size of the residential house seems inadequate to accommodate the whole family, but as a rule nobody even thinks about the possibility of occupying the larger one that stands vacant nearby. The latter is called *"casa mare"* (literally "big house" in Romanian) and is normally used for storing things that belonged to the *ancestors* of the family—their clothes, bedlinen, crockery and cutlery, jewelry, photographs, smoking pipes, snuffboxes, walking sticks, and anything else they kept (but maybe never used) in their lifetime and bequeathed to posterity. The rational motivation for that custom is that it that the stored things are supposed to become the dowry for the female offspring of that family. In actual fact, whenever a girl from the family gets married, she simply moves her share in the ancestral possessions to her new home to be stored in the *casa mare* of the recipient family.

I think that nowhere else can we observe the veneration of ancestors so clearly as in this example. Although a thoroughly Christian nation, the

Moldovans respect their ancestors so much that they allocate them the more spacious place, which is much better stocked with valuables than the one used by the living. I can only add that this practice completely survived during the period of communist rule (1940–91) and was even publicized as a typical manifestation of traditional culture—for, unlike religion which was discouraged by the Soviets, everything "ethnic" was usually kept under their patronage (provided that it did not look too religious). The Christian church finds nothing wrong with this form of veneration either—the tradition is too deep-rooted to make any attempts to rethink or revise it.

I am aware that in some parts of Africa it is (was) common to erect shrines in honor of ancestors and that those shrines usually resemble human habitations. However, I also know that they are typically much smaller in size and have only a token material value. Apparently, the Moldovans take the living conditions of their ancestors much more seriously, even though nowadays all this is done on a subconscious level and by no means sanctified by the dominant religion. The "sacrifices" thus tendered to ancestors are out of all proportion, even by the standards of Africa where the progenitors would be normally offered a symbolic share in the family's meal only.

It remains for me to say that the only occasion on which one has a chance to stay in the *casa mare* is when the number of the family's visitors on a particular night is too large to attempt squeezing them all into the main residential building. In that case, some of them (but only as a last resort) can actually be placed in the ancestral house. A couple of times it has happened to me. I must say that sleeping in a place like that feels like a completely unworldly experience. The *casa mare* is usually never heated, even in winter, as it normally stays unoccupied. Because it gets so thoroughly frozen in winter, it never manages to properly "thaw" for the rest of the year, even in summer. When you stay there, it breathes sepulchral cold upon you. The furniture is rarely dusted and everything smells moldy. You are surrounded by pictures of the family's forebears—the only company you are allowed to keep in that house. There is no better place to get in touch with them now and again than the *casa mare*.

How far the Catholic Church would be prepared to follow the above example, i.e. tolerate certain extreme forms of veneration, I cannot tell. One thing is however quite certain: The more inclusivist a solution is, the more effort it will require on the Christian part to analyze, understand, adapt to, and (to the greatest possible extent) adopt local traditions which often look incompatible with Christianity but which, on closer look, may be expected to diversify and enrich it. How adequate the Catholic Church is to that task is, once again, beyond my modest means to answer. Still less do I dare speculate what practical form that eventual symbiosis could take and whether the creed that would ultimately develop from it would not appear as something like this:

"We believe in the Holy Ghost that proceeds from our ancestors

"And in our Lord Jesus Christ who, being Son of God, waived His right to become an ancestor for the sake of saving the whole mankind.

"He died young, thus acquiring to power to serve all the nations.

"He was brought to Africa by white people who had first murdered Him but who, nevertheless, could neither hide him, nor prevent him from relocation to Africa. Amen."

Chapter XVII

Pluralism

FROM A PURELY SECULAR point of view, pluralism is the best and easiest solution to the problem of interreligious relations. Without going into theological niceties, it proceeds on the assumption that all forms of religious consciousness (including atheism) must enjoy equal rights and avoid confrontation. Moreover, secularism, in its advanced forms, does not merely stop at providing equal treatment to different manifestations of religion but also cares for maintaining the diversity of the spiritual environment in any given society, much in the same way as it is aimed at maintaining a similar balance of the natural ecosystems with which that society interacts. From secular perspective, it may be just as important that a particular species of religion does not overturn the balance within the noosphere, as it is important to prevent a certain biological species from infinitely dominating the rest. Such domination, as we know from ecology, will be eventually detrimental not only to the species considered to be endangered but also to the dominating species itself. In other words, viewed secularly, the global environmental disaster currently underway on our planet due to the excessive dominance of Homo Sapiens is paralleled by the spiritual disaster caused by the monotheistic religions endangering the existence of the traditional ones.

However, secularism does not seem to be a suitable solution for modern Africa which remains predominantly religious in its ways of thinking and acting. If any pluralism is at all possible on that continent, it would have to originate from monotheists themselves (Christians and Muslims in the first place) in whose power it is currently either to wipe off the last remnants of traditionalism or to take steps towards its preservation, or, as it would be more appropriate to say in this instance, its *conservation* which can ultimately turn out to be in the monotheists' own interests.

How realistic is that prospect? Its theological basis certainly exists. Many Christian writers (with John Hick as possibly the best-known example) have gone far enough to promote very liberal ecumenical ideas. It is true that they do not belong to mainstream Christianity and that almost none of them are based in Africa. However, with other things being equal, it should be only a matter of time for their ideas to receive wider circulation and establish bridgeheads in Africa. And yet, even if the possibility of such a development cannot be completely excluded, one must still be aware that it may have no better chance of practical success than the policy of inculturation which has been largely at a standstill in spite of being officially adopted and promoted by the Catholic Church. For it can quickly face similar, if not more difficult, semiotic obstacles as those be touched upon in the previous chapters.

In this chapter we are going to consider some of these obstacles, bearing in mind that their actual number is much greater.

1. Progress vs Conservatism

The predominant mode of signifying our modern attitude to past and present is based on the idea of progress. Viewed in this manner, any event in the history of mankind constitutes a forward movement. Any technological invention, for example, is supposed to supersede the previously existing "state of the art" and make our life more efficient and better organized. Any religion (or denial of all religion) that succeeds a previous religious system is, from the same point a view, a step forward, towards a better organized relationship between man and God. Thus, any pre-Christian form of religion would be necessarily viewed as something inferior, less efficient and less developed. Even though it may still be supposed to contain certain positive values, it would be nevertheless always "evil" compared to the superior system that comes to replace it.

However, from the semiotic point of view, it is only one of the possible perspectives which can be easily reversed. The picture it presents can be changed to the negative and thus suggest very different conclusions. Theoretically at least, such an alternative system of coordinates can be just as valid as the one that currently predominates the views shared by the majority.

From this alternative perspective, any forward movement can be regarded as further departure from the original state of perfection, as violation of the pristine harmony, as a step towards the final disintegration and collapse that awaits any progress. More efficient technology, for example, can often imply designing more efficient weapons which, in turn, can ultimately cause mankind's self-destruction in a global armed conflict. From this viewpoint, absolute monotheism can result in man's complete reliance on God's will, which, in turn, could cause man's loss of his own free will. But the latter can be destructive for man's ability to choose between good and evil; can, in other words, result in his reversion back to animality and impossibility to make responsible decisions in assuring his salvation.

Viewed in less eschatological terms, progress can be interpreted as a sign of spiritual deterioration. Indeed, even in the fairy recent past, technology, in most cases, could be still under control of single individuals who could reproduce all the stages of a process without relying on the knowledge of those they would never communicate with. A primitive agriculturalist, for example, was able to procure the seed stock for the upcoming sowing season, to manufacture the necessary tools for the operations he was about to perform, to procure the natural fertilizers and to harvest the crop, being thus ready to repeat the cycle next season. A primitive religionist, in a very similar manner, would know all the necessary rites and spells to assure his favorable treatment on the part of the deity. Traditional religion is actually a collection of such spiritual "flowcharts" which are based on millennial experience and which therefore will not admit any deviation from the established procedure, just in the same way as deviation from a technical protocol would result in a failure to accomplish a set process.

In modern society, however, such self-reliance is no longer possible. A modern worker has in most cases to rely on other people's technological achievements which he is unable to reproduce independently. From this point of view, he is thus less intelligent than his primitive predecessor because he has to apply the technology uncritically, mechanically, without proper understanding "how things work." A modern religionist is, similarly, entirely at deity's mercy—all communication with the spiritual world goes in one direction. He is always a passive recipient of divine grace; he has no right to demand an explanation why he has to act in the prescribed way and whether it is really the best way for him.

An entire dependence of third-party technology can ultimately lead to a situation where even a minor corruption in a single link of the "supply chain" will render the process inefficient, even useless. It is also possible that the general progress of humanity can reach such a critical point where the integrity of that chain would be lost to a disastrous effect. In a situation like that, the whole development would revert to a stage where that chain still remains functional. That means, in fact, that the bearers of traditional integral knowledge would have an obvious advantage over those who rely on ready-made solutions. The latter, on the other hand, would be rendered completely helpless.

From this reverse perspective, translated into religious idiom, we can say that Doomsday should be expected at the point where people's reliance on the omniscient deity will be so absolute, as to preclude any critical questioning of the divine plan; where the righteous will adhere to their righteousness and the sinners persevere in their sinfulness (assuming that their sinning is also directed by divine providence) to such an extent that no alternative arrangement will be any longer possible. This point would signify a completion of the divine plan, as both the righteous and the sinful would constitute isolated pools, separated by a gulf (Luke 16:26), with no interchange possible between the two sectors. It will only remain for the deity to assign these two pools to their respective destinations—heaven and hell—for the ages of ages.

I want to emphasize that the above considerations are purely semiotic in nature; the actual state of things is more complicated and that the hypothetical interreligious dialogue that may be conducted on the basis of pluralism can result of the appearance of such religious forms which would present a certain combination of traditionalist and Christian views that would result in an outcome other than the one that would precipitate a collapse of civilization and restoration of primal animism. I only wanted to point out the fact that such a dialogue would have to be conducted from diametrically opposed positions with regard to the understanding of development and progress.

I would like to end this section with an example which will, hopefully, add some life to my otherwise lifeless speculations. This time it will again come from my personal experience.

Case Study 7. The Cellar and the Cell Phone

During our second trip to Africa, we made it as far as the Upper West Region of Ghana, to visit the Wechiau Community Hippo Sanctuary. On our visit we were accompanied by a charming local volunteer whose name has unfortunately slipped out of my memory. Closer to the end of our staying at Wechiau, our guide and I were exchanging some brief remarks regarding the lifestyle of local people. The question that bothered me was why it was not common among the Africans to have cellars at their houses. Considering the hot climate in which they lived, I thought it would be a helpful improvement as it would allow local residents to preserve their foods in a more efficient manner. My suggestion was, in fact, based on my Moldovan background, as in my native land every rural house usually comes with a cellar where almost all household's victuals are stored.

My companion did not seem to have an answer to that question. All that he managed to say in reply was that while cellars are unknown in Africa, it must be for a reason. He did not know what that reason could be and did not seem to care to know, because, he said, as long as his ancestors used to live that way, their rightness must not to put in doubt.

Thus spoke my guide, while holding a mobile phone in his hand. I said nothing in response but I thought it nonetheless strange that someone inclined to follow the way of his ancestors did not mind using a device completely unknown to them.

I kept coming back in my thoughts to this brief conversation long after we left the Upper West Region. I would ask myself why one technical innovation ran contrary to ancestral customs but not the other one. It finally occurred to me that the two things were of a different kind. A cellar is a technology that everyone can understand and critically evaluate. If a certain society has not come up with it, that must be for a reason that can be ascertained. This reason can be either economic or religious in nature, or both. (As it is the case, for example, with the prohibition of pork in Judaism and Islam: Is it purely religious or does it have hygienic considerations added to it?)

The mobile phone is a completely different thing. No one knows how it works and as such it is not perceived as a piece of technology but as a purely miraculous object. Its miraculous nature is the best argument for its uncritical adoption. The ancestors are not competent to decide how appropriate it is. It is adopted as a gift from overseas, it is extraneous to the native system of values, it comes to replace the latter as obsolete, not to reform it.

In a similar way, Christianity (and Islam) are often viewed as miraculous means of salvation which, although impenetrable in their mechanism of action, are found to be more efficient than the traditional ones. Connecting to a friend with a single touch of a button on an imported device is just as miraculous and efficient as obtaining salvation by a single calling the name of a foreign deity.

2. Plenitude vs Deficiency

Another critical difference between the modes of religious signification in African Traditional Religion and Christianity concerns two very different types of symbolism.

It is common knowledge that the idea of God is often associated with that of completeness, fulness, plenitude, pleroma—anything that suggests the divine all-in-all. An unbroken circle, an equilateral triangle, a well-proportioned building or a human figure—all these symbols can be suitable designations of the Supreme Being because they suggest the idea of perfection and self-sufficiency.

However, a certain stage of religious development may witness the appearance of such symbols which reflect the idea of God *by contrast*. In this case, the symbol will emphasize how imperfect the earthly things are compared to divine fulness; how meagre, lopsided, flawed, and dark they look compared to the divine brightness and symmetry. From this point of view, the less the signifier resembles its signified, the more adequately it expresses it, the more easily can the divine shine on us through the ragged and patched fabric of the earthly being. The more deficiency it displays, the more adequately it may reveal the divine plenitude. An arc, an asymmetric shape, circumcision, castration, an emaciated body, a shabby hut, a half-erased word, a homeless person—all these can serve as symbolic means to render that idea.

It would be a simplification to say that traditional religions favor the first type of symbolism, while Christianity does the second one. Indeed, Christianity has made use of many symbols it inherited from predecessor religions which are based on the idea of plenitude, rather than deficiency. Yet its most essential symbols often point in the opposite direction. Its chief image is that of Christ, injured and insulted, bleeding and groaning. His soul is about to part with his body which cannot hold it anymore. Even in his lifetime he was nothing but a homeless tramp who did not know where to lay his head (Matt 8:20). The chief way of imitating Christ is asceticism, i.e. posing as a living sign of dearth and imbalance—in anticipation and manifestation of the plenitude and equipoise to be acquired in afterlife.

It is not that such type of symbolism is unknown to Africa. As we noted in previous chapters, many of its fetishes, idols, and shrines may look asymmetrical, rough, unsteady or imbalanced. It is a matter of complete incompatibility but that of partial overlap. Nowhere else, in my opinion, is this discrepancy clearer than in the semiotic aspects of things that involve man's lifestyle. The poor are "blessed" in Christianity but not in Africa. It is true that in everyday practice Christians tend to ignore that beatitude every now and then but, while doing so, at least some of them are aware that such behavior may involve repercussions in the fulness of time. Christianity is a religion that assigns a positive value to pain and suffering. From that point of view, it has simply failed its mission in Africa because it did not manage to convert the excessive suffering on that continent (of which a significant part was brought simultaneously with the new religion) into something just as positive. The current suffering of Africa is not perceived as something that contributes to its higher stature or its brighter future, as something which lays the foundation of upcoming prosperity. Is it all because Christianity is simply incapable of accomplishing such a mission, being too much oriented towards the other world? I shall not venture an answer this question but I can only again point out how difficult it may be for Christianity to justify its presence in Africa if it agrees to proceed on the assumptions of enlightened pluralism.

3. Linearity vs Circularity

It is also commonly stated that the African traditional model of social life is predominantly cyclic, while the model brought by Christians is mostly linear. As a result an alien idea of irreversible development was imposed on Africa with negative consequences. Yet, all that is not always quite so simple.

First of all, Christianity is largely a cyclic notion too. Its daily life is built around the liturgical year with its invariable change of seasons which, in their turn, are grouped around the events of Jesus' life. As such, it is a purely cyclic model. It is true, of course, that all this is viewed as only a temporary arrangement that must give way to Parousia which is expected to usher in a new creation. However, the little that the Christians have been told about the world to come (mostly in the Book of Revelation) allows them to suppose that the future life is also expected to be organized around a liturgical cycle, the only difference with the previous arrangement being that all the uncertainties of the old creation will then be resolved and all obstacles cleared. The modern belief in indefinite progress, as we have seen in the previous section, is not an originally Christian idea, even though nowadays many Christians seem to subscribe to it. The source of that idea may rather lie in the opposition between the rural and urban culture, where the former is totally dependent on the nature's cycle and the latter cares almost nothing for it. From that perspective, the higher the urbanization of a particular society is, the higher the dominance of the thought patterns that suggest the idea of linearity.

African religion certainly does not envision a transition from present to future in terms of such a revolutionary calamity, as Christianity does, but this may be because it does not perceive such enormous resistance to the will of God on the part of evil powers as Christianity does. Other than that, the general indifference of African religions towards the future can be explained by the fact that the Africans tend to emphasize the similarity between the old and new arrangements of the world, while Christianity is prone to highlight the abrupt transition from one to the other.

Besides, the Kingdom of God which Christianity expects to set in after the end of this world may not look as attractive to an African traditionalist, considering that the number of those to be fully saved may, in fact, be very limited. What if proper salvation is actually reserved only for those "an hundred forty and four thousand" who "were not defiled with women" (Rev 14:1–4)? There is simply no way to disprove that statement or to prohibit its literal reading. With Revelation being the concluding book of the biblical canon, it remains possible that as such it presents the final word of Christianity regarding the fate of everyone. There is no way either to oppose the numerous inferences that can be made from this statement, including the most inhumane ideas of Calvinism which teaches that salvation is entirely beyond human control.

Would any African be happy with such a Kingdom the access to which will be most likely denied him because his primary concern (at least until recently) has been to produce offspring which has no other way to effect but to "defile" oneself with a woman?

Once again, however, I want to stop short of getting theological, rather than merely semiotic. All I wanted to highlight in this section was the same pluralistic predicament—the anticipation that Christianity may find it very hard to engage with traditional religion if it is indeed prepared to treat the latter as an equal partner in dialogue, rather than an inferior form of consciousness which the former is free to destroy or preserve.

I hope the reader will agree with me now that pluralism is the least explored and the most arduous-looking option, which will require both radical reshuffling of the Christian doctrine and no less radical resignation of its allegedly exceptional place among the other religions. Yet even if theological compatibility is theoretically possible, the semiotic incompatibility of different traditions may look insurmountable. This is why I did not want to offer any systematic comparison but rather limited myself to outlining a few almost random issues that can hopefully allow the reader to form an idea about the nature of the problem. I refrain from any other conclusions until I am through with my last case study.

Case Study 8. The Fada

The advantage of fiction is that it often expresses relatively concisely those ideas that may take many pages and even whole chapters in a standard philosophic treatise. My readers may also remember that I have a literary background and therefore feel more at home while analyzing works of fiction, rather than purely theoretical expostulations. This is the reason why I want to finish my book with a reading from a modern Ghanaian writer, Monsignor Raphael Owusu Peprah, whose short novel *Stranded on Both Banks* (first published in 2010) contains, in my opinion, a very representative version of the problem which also constitutes the main subject of my book—the relationship between African Traditional Religion and Christianity. It is only one of the few problems that the author tackles in his novel but it is certainly the one that occupies its climax (chapters 12–13, 18–25, 31 in the 2015 Student Edition).[1]

The story is told by Juni, a young boy who has just turned thirteen and who lives in Kumasi with his mother and five more children. The mother has to raise all of them on her own as her husband (a former university professor) is a political émigré who lives in the United States. The family is Catholic and is often visited by their priest and friend whom they simply call "Fada" (which reflects the local pronunciation of "Father"). The time setting is probably the 1970s (the book mentions video games as a still relatively unknown thing among Ghanaian children).

To celebrate Juni's birthday, Mammy suggests traveling to Fada's native village of Duakese which is situated in some distance from Kumasi, deep in the jungle. Juni likes that place so much that he wants to stay on for another couple of days. He is allowed to do so, while the rest of his family leave the village.

During his stay, Juni makes friends with four local boys. He learns from them that there is a Sacred Forest in the vicinity, with a Sacred Tree growing in the middle. He wants to visit that forest and the local boys (with the exception of one) think it a good idea. After a rather difficult journey, the party manages to reach the Sacred Tree. Suddenly one of boys (one with an urban background) snatches a cutlass from his comrade and makes a deep gash in the tree (it remains unexplained why he does so). What happens next can be interpreted as a vengeful reaction of the spiritual powers to the act of desecration committed by that boy. A strong gust of wind almost immediately follows his wounding the tree.

In two days' time, the village experiences a short but extremely destructive rainfall with a hurricane. It inflicts a devastating damage on many buildings. To boot, an elderly villager is killed by lightning. The anxious residents are starting to search for the cause of the disaster that has befallen them. Then the boy who slashed the Sacred Tree goes down with malaria.

---

1. I have a copy of that book in my possession thanks to the pains taken by Comfort Appiah who dutifully traced, bought, and shipped it to me in the UK—a feat of enormous importance, considering the role this book was going to play in my analysis.

The other boys who accompanied him (but not Juni) are now suspecting that the disaster may be down to their recently committed sacrilege and confess to their trespass.

The elders and traditional priests are now convinced that the boys are the actual culprits who by their irresponsible behavior have called down the wrath of local gods and ancestors. They want to proceed with propitiatory rites but in order to do that they must first obtain Fada's support (both moral and material). They come into his house, stating their grievances and demands, the main one being the need to provide the material (animals, etc.) to perform a sacrifice. However, Fada tries to convince them that their efforts are misdirected. He launches the following passionate tirade in support of his views:

> 'Allegedly, the desecration of the Sacred Tree by unfledged children angered the gods and ancestors of the land. Consequently, acting in concert, they have punished the entire village with a turbulent storm which has destroyed life and property. The sages have said that if one chews one's own tongue because of an uncontrolled appetite for meat, that person has certainly not consumed the best of meat because it is a muscle. Invariably, the ravenous desire would starve the person to death in the absence of the tongue. Hence, by engaging in a fratricidal war and thereby destroying their own kith and kin to appease themselves, the gods and ancestors have done nothing remarkable other than destroying themselves. Will the gods and ancestors be pleased to see their own underprivileged kinfolk bereft of shelter, food and peace? Certainly they are not sadistic to leave their own royals in such suffering and quandary. When a combination of extreme anger and disdain drives you to hit hard the fly sitting on your sore, you will end up exacerbating the condition of the sore. If the spirits love their grand and great grandchildren they will ignore the blunders of innocent children. Are the spirits intensely insensitive to human suffering? Are they so disingenuous? Should the gods and ancestors not know that these boys did what they did unsuspectingly? Unfortunately, luck did not smile on their trip. Is there no compassion and forgiveness being shown by the gods and ancestors? No pity? No mercy?'

In the above speech, Fada, to the best of his abilities, does his own bit of "inculturation." He seems to admit (or at least pretends to admit) the existence of traditional gods and ancestral spirits. However, having acknowledged their reality, he immediately goes into the offensive by trying to show that those deities are irrational and self-destructive as they seem to punish the villagers whom they are supposed to protect—only because an act of disrespect has been committed against them by a few children who were not perfectly aware of what they were doing. It is perfectly clear from which position Fada argues his case: he opposes the all-forgiving Christian God to the legalistic and vengeful deities of traditional religion.

Yet Fada's case may not be so strong as it appears at first sight. Ultimately, as it often happens with monotheistic religions, it can all be reduced to the question of theodicy. Within the traditional system both responsibility and control are clearly assigned to and distributed among the respective parties. The deities are responsible for patronizing the village by assuring its wellbeing. The village inhabitants are responsible for maintaining those deities by sharing with them a token part of their produce and by strictly observing all rites and taboos on which their relationship with the deities rests. Should any villager deviate—deliberately or unintentionally—from the established code of practice, the whole community becomes responsible for his act and must take prompt steps to rectify the wrong by offering propitiatory sacrifices to the deities. Should the community fail to act towards placating the deities, the latter will be free to take punitive measures with respect to the villagers by castigating them with diseases and natural disasters. In both cases (compliance and non-compliance) it is the deities who are in full control of the village's bliss or woe.

Within the Christian system, things look much more uncertain. Christianity (at least in the version professed by Fada) cannot give a definite answer to the question why a disaster has overtaken the village, why one of its residents (and no other one) has been killed by lightning and why some of the children (but not the other ones) have contracted malaria. All these misfortunes are broadly classed as accidents and/or natural occurrences. The question, however, arises, who is in control of all these events. If they proceed from God, His motivation is unclear: Why should He punish the villagers who live in abject poverty or a supposedly innocent boy who committed his transgression unawares? If they do not proceed from God but rather happen "by chance" why does God remain withdrawn, while injustice is being perpetrated in a world under His responsibility? Finally, if God's actions are fair, although incomprehensible, why does Fada not accept them as such but instead counteracts them by rushing the sick boy to hospital? Or, if he does find them unfair, why does he not try to change the course of events by simply praying for the boy's health? Or does he rely more on the miracles of western medicine than on God's supernatural assistance? Is western medicine the only way to combat the evil? Can it be then that the God which Fada professes is not really the Christian God but the God-of-the-gaps of the late nineteenth century or a deistic deity of European

Enlightenment who, similarly to the Supreme Being of many African Religions, remains withdrawn from the daily fuss of human affairs?

I am not demanding any immediate answers to the questions above. Once again, I am not a theologian to engage in that sort of discussion. But one does not even have to be theologian to realize how much more difficult it is for a monotheistic religion to explain the existence of evil than for a traditional religion. Christianity should certainly be ready to face these questions if it really wants to engage in dialogue with traditionalism on the basis of pluralism. On the other hand, if it is determined to maintain the posture of the only true religion, it may not have to trouble itself with questions like those.

It is, however, fair to say that Fada's version of Christianity is not the only one depicted in the novel. The alternative is presented by a certain sect that runs the "Jerusalem Prayer Camp" on the outskirts of the village. They obviously practice a syncretic cult as they believe that the boy's illness has been caused by witchcraft. They, at least, believe that they can cure him by calling Jesus for help and expelling Satan as the enemy. This is obvious from the text of the novel, even though the whole scene at the prayer camp is painted in unmistakably caricature colors:

> Some of the members held their hands up and moved them wildly like they were conjuring some super natural [sic] powers. In a kind of frenzy, the rest frowned and moved their bodies likes [sic] snakes slithering along. They were drumming, singing and praying. Their words were mumbled, utterly unintelligible, yet forceful and compelling. However, I heard two words distinctly—Jesus and Satan. They stamped their feet heavily on the floor at the mention of Satan and raised their hands high up at the mention of Jesus. They continued rattling prayers, damning Satan, praising Jesus and literally instructing Jesus to heal Hammer [the sick boy] who looked weak.

Once again, the Catholic Church should probably be prepared to answer the question, whose version of Christianity looks more convincing: its own that relies entirely on modern pharmaceutics or the more traditional one, with its greater emphasis on faith healing. The question is becoming increasingly topical if we consider the speedy progress of Charismatic Christianity in the recent decades—that version of Christianity which specifically relies on the power of faith in treating bodily ailments. Would the Catholic approach also look like a caricature from the perspective of this increasingly popular branch of Christianity in Africa? Is Pentecostalism the only realistic way to preserve at least some links with the traditional past or can we hope that pluralism may strengthen its positions in the foreseeable future? Time will tell, perhaps.

But where is the semiotics of it all?—my readers may ask. It comes later, in chapter 31, after Fada, under the influence of his colleague and ex-schoolmate Frank, slightly modifies his stance and yields to the elders' demands. The friends then start a general conversation about the prospects of indigenous religion and the following opinion is voiced:

> 'Frank, we must bear the onus of discerning the religious aspects and the cultural values from the spurious ones. It is time to *decipher* the *beautiful* traditional and cultural values from those *dangerous* and *hostile* rituals and practices,' Fada said.

I have highlighted the key words in the quotation below, which make a good representation of Fada's semiotic thinking. By using the word "decipher" he correctly identifies the relationship between "cultural values" and "rituals/practices" as that between the signified and the signifier: we understand the values of a given religion by observing (or participating in) its rights and customs, which allows us to read ("decipher") their meaning. Yet, in Fada's opinion, while those values are "beautiful," their means of expression are "dangerous" and "hostile." Does it mean then that they are inadequate in their signification? If so, how can something which is dangerous and hostile to the observer express something which is essentially beneficial? Does Christianity provide a better signification for the same ideas or does it express different ideas because its means of expression are "safer" and "friendlier"? These questions remain unanswered, partly because Fada's semiotics is far from being consistent. As such, it probably reflects the inconsistent position of the Catholic Church as a whole on this subject. Will it manage to overcome this inconsistency in the near future?

Conclusion

To put it in strictly "scientific" terms, this book can be summarized in the following two sentences: Christianity's renewal message which ultimately derives from the Jewish priority of the graphic sign over the oral one, finds a favorable environment for propagation in Africa due to the absence of an established written tradition on one hand and due to the presence of nearly identical patterns of religious signification on the other. However, some points of semiotic incompatibility between the two religious traditions can be identified, which eventually lead to the question whether the universal adoption of monotheism means, summarily, spiritual enrichment or spiritual impoverishment for that continent.

From Christian perspective, however, this conclusion will look relevant only if we adopt the pluralistic attitude to the problem of interfaith relations in Africa and worldwide. Religious pluralism is certainly the preferred option for anyone who approaches the subject from secularist positions (the author of this book included). Yet secularism is not professed by the majority of Africans, which makes the prospects of that ideology uncertain on that continent. Consequently, just as uncertain are the prospects that African Traditional Religion will be treated by Africans themselves as a spiritual asset whose value is not inferior or at least is not completely covered by Christianity.

Nevertheless, most modern African countries are officially secular societies whose governments are supposed to be responsible not only for guaranteeing equal rights to different religions but also for maintaining cultural diversity and preservation of Africa's cultural heritage to the fullest possible extent. The latter certainly means taking conscious steps towards conservation of Africa's traditional religions. In practice, however, the question is: How far is Africa (as well as the world community) prepared to invest in solutions to assure that conservation? We can take a step further and put a more global question: How much is Africa ready to assume the role of an active participant in the battle of spirituality against the soullessness of modern civilization?

As we have seen from the last three chapters, the answers will depend on the goodwill on many parties involved and the choices they will make. There are certainly more and less expensive options ranging from "do-nothing" scenarios and quick fixes to large-scale campaigns aimed at maintaining Africa's cultural uniqueness. In all cases, irrespective of the choice, the role of Christianity is critical. The actual outcome may depend not only on Christendom's willingness to reconsider its own stance, to overcome its superiority complex and to prioritize similarities, rather than differences, with other religions. Yet, even if the most pluralistic approach is chosen (which is highly unlikely in the present circumstances) all this may not be sufficient on its own to turn the tide of current religious trends. The interreligious dialogue, in order to be successful, would require involvement of all social powers, both governmental and non-governmental ones.

This includes both financial support and establishment of a proper intellectual base that would produce competent advocates of traditionalism. Unlike monotheistic religions, traditional religions are very limited in their funding opportunities and should be granted official sponsorship—just like many other things that to not belong to the mainstream. The crucial question in that respect is whether Africa possesses the necessary resources to accomplish that mission. The specific answer to that question will vary, of course, from country to country. Unexpected as it may sound, the viability of African Traditional Religion is largely dependent of Africa's economic performance in the coming decades.

This conclusion may look appallingly Marxist to some of my readers as well as to myself. What else is it but Marxism, to make the development of religion conditional on economic prosperity? Well, perhaps it is not so surprising, considering the thoroughly Marxist upbringing I received in my formative years, both at school and at university, having grown up in a society whose official ideology was economic materialism and atheism—the now defunct Soviet Union. In that respect, my situation may mirror that of the atheists who had a thorough religious upbringing in their childhood and early youth and who (as we saw in one of the chapters) in spite of all their efforts to the contrary, cannot help expressing their nihilistic views in terms of positive religion. Yet I also think that it is always preferable to drift towards spiritualizing matter than to travel in the opposite direction—to debase spirit by reducing it to material components.

Neither do I think that religion is opium for people, as Marx did. On the contrary, I believe it to be an integral part of our consciousness—whether we like to acknowledge it or not; whether or not we begin our day with offering thanks to the Supreme Being. I sincerely hope that this book has managed to make it clear.

Bibliography

African Traditional Religions in Contemporary Society, edited by Jacob K. Olupona, Paragon House, 1991.
Augustine of Hippo. *The City of God*, translated by Rev Marcus Dodds, Xist Publishing, 2015.
Bempah, Kofi. *Akan Traditional Religion: The Myths and The Truth*, BookSurge Publishing, 2010.
Cassirer, Ernst. *Language and Myth*, Dover Publications, 2003.
———. *The Philosophy of Symbolic Forms*, 3 vols, Yale University Press, 1955–1957.
Christaller, J. G. *A collection of 3,600 Tshi Proverbs In Use Among the Africans of the Gold Coast as Speaking the Asante and Fante Language, Collected, Together with their Variations, and Alphabetically Arranged*, Edwin Mellen Press, 1990.
Cobley, Paul and Litza, Jansz. *Introducing Semiotics: A Graphic Guide*, Icon Books Ltd., Kindle Edition.
Danquah, J.B. *The Akan Doctrine of God*, Routledge, second edition, 1968.
Dawkins, Richard. *The God Delusion*, Transworld Publishers, second edition, 2018.
Derrida, Jacque. *Of Grammatology*, translated by Gayatri Chakravorty Spivak, The John Hopkins University Press, 1976.
Diogenes Laërtius, *Lives and Opinions of Eminent Philosophers*, Project Gutenberg, http://www.gutenberg.org/files/57342/57342-h/57342-h.htm.
Ephirim-Donkor, Anthony. *African Personality and Spirituality: The Role of Abosom and Human Essence*, Lexington Books, 2016.
Eusebius of Caesarea. *Preparation for the Gospel*, translated by E. H. Gifford, 1903, transcribed by Roger Pearse, Ipswich, UK, 2003 (downloadable as a pdf file).
Evans-Pritchard, E. E. *Witchcraft, Oracles and Magic Among the Azande*, abridged with an introduction by Eva Gillies, Clarendon Press, 1976.
Frazer, James George. The Golden Bough, Project Gutenberg, 2003, http://www.gutenberg.org/files/3623/3623-h/3623-h.htm.
———. *Folk-lore in the Old Testament*, Kindle Edition.
Fretheim, Sara J. *Kwame Bediako and African Christian Scholarship: Emerging Religious Discourse in Twentieth-Century Ghana*, Pickwick Publications, Kindle Edition, 2018.
Freud, Sigmund. *Totem and Taboo*, translated by A.A. Brill, Neeland Media LLC. 2009, Kindle Edition.
Harris, J. Rendel. *Boanerges*, Forgotten Books, 2017.
Idowu, E. Bọlaji. *Olódùmarè: God in Yoruba Belief*, Longmans, 1962.

Kierkegaard, Søren, *Fear and Trembling*, translated by Walter Lowrie, Princeton University Press, 1941, http://www.religion-online.org/book-chapter/chapter-3-problem-one-is-there-such-a-thing-as-a-teleological-suspension-of-the-ethical/.

Kuma, Afua. *Jesus of the Deep Forest: Prayers and Praises of Afua Kuma*, translated by Jon Kirby, Asempa, 1981.

Fretheim, Sara J. Kwame Bediako and African Christian Scholarship: Emerging Religious Discourse in Twentieth-Century Ghana (African Christian Studies Series Book 13) . Pickwick Publications, an Imprint of Wipf and Stock Publishers. Kindle Edition.

Lévy-Bruhl, Lucien. *How Natives Think*, translated by Lilian A. Claire, Martino Fine Books, Kindle Edition, 2015.

Lévy-Strauss, Claude. *Structural Anthropology*, translated by Claire Jacobson and Brooke Grundfest Schoepf, Doubleday Anchor Books, 1967.

Lonergan, Bernard. *Method in Theology*, University of Toronto Press, 2013.

Nietzsche, Friedrich. *Early Greek Philosophy & Other Essays*, translated by Maximilian A. Mügge, The Macmillan Company, 1911, https://www.gutenberg.org/files/51548/51548-h/51548-h.htm.

Orji, Cyril. *A Semiotic Approach to the Theology of Inculturation*, Pickwick Publications, Kindle Edition, 2015.

Peirce, Charles Sanders. *Peirce on Signs*, The University of North Carolina Press, 1991, Kindle Edition.

Pentecostalism and Witchcraft: Spiritual Warfare in Africa and Melanesia, edited by Knut Rio, Michelle MacCarthy and Ruy Blanes, Palgrave Macmillan, 2017.

Peprah, Monsignor Raphael Owusu. *Stranded on Both Banks*, Ankof Ventures, 2015.

Rattray, R.S. *Ashanti*, Oxford University Press, 1923.

———. *Religion & Art in Ashanti*, Oxford University Press, 1927.

Sarpong, Peter K. *Peoples Differ: An Approach to Inculturation in Evangelisation*, Sub-Saharan Publishers, 2002.

Saussure, Ferdinand de, *Course in General Linguistics*, translated and annotated by Roy Harris, Duckworth, 1983.

Two Say Why, Search Press Ltd, 1972.

Tylor, Edward. *Primitive Culture*, 2 vols, Dover Publications, 2016.

Vico, Giambattista. *New Science*, translated by David Marsh, Penguin Books, Kindle Edition.

Yell, Robert A. *Semiotics of Religion: Signs of the Sacred in History*, Bloomsbury Publishing, 2013.

www.ingramcontent.com/pod-product-compliance
Lightning Source LLC
Chambersburg PA
CBHW050825160426
43192CB00010B/1895